FROM FINALS TO THE FIRM

THE TOP TEN THINGS NEW ASSOCIATES NEED TO KNOW

Including a Bonus Chapter Exclusively for Summer Associates

EXPANDED SECOND EDITION

By

Calvin Gladney, Esq.
and
Raymond Millien, Esq.

WEST®

A Thomson Reuters business

Mat #40859283

© 2009 Thomson Reuters

    610 Opperman Drive
    St. Paul, MN 55123
    1–800–313–9378

Printed in the United States of America

ISBN: 978–0–314–90427–0

ABOUT THE AUTHORS

CALVIN GLADNEY, LEED AP, is a recovering attorney and is Managing Partner of Mosaic Urban Partners, LLC, a real estate development and advisory services firm based in Washington, D.C. Mosaic's core purpose is to transform urban communities.

Prior to founding Mosaic, Mr. Gladney served as Vice President of the Anacostia Waterfront Corporation (AWC), a quasi-public real estate corporation chartered by the District of Columbia. Prior to joining AWC, Mr. Gladney was General Counsel and Transactions Manager at BRIDGE Housing Corporation, a private real estate developer in San Francisco, CA. Prior to his tenure at BRIDGE, Mr. Gladney was the first Counsel and Senior Development Director at the National Capital Revitalization Corporation (NCRC), a quasi-public corporation chartered by the District of Columbia, where he provided legal and strategic advice to the CEO. Prior to his tenure at NCRC, Mr. Gladney was a transactional real estate attorney at Latham & Watkins in Washington, D.C., where he was the lead attorney on a variety of real estate acquisitions and refinancings. During law school, he was a summer associate at Hogan and Hartson LLP in Washington, DC and clered at Olshan, Grundman, Frome & Rosenzweig, a corporate and securities boutique located in New York City.

Mr. Gladney graduated *cum laude* from Harvard Law School and received his Bachelor of Science from Cornell University. He is admitted to the bar in the District of Columbia, California and New York. Mr. Gladney also is a LEED Accredited Professional. He is a member of the Executive Committee of the Urban Land Institute's Washington, D.C. District Council, the Sustainable Business Network of Washington, D.C. and the DC Building Industry Association.

RAYMOND MILLIEN was previously General Counsel of OCEAN TOMO, LLC, responsible for overseeing all legal and regulatory affairs, as well as assisting the firm's management with acquisitions and the structuring of joint ventures. Prior to that, he was VP and Group IP Counsel at AMERICAN EXPRESS COMPANY where his responsibilities included managing the company's global patent portfolio and leading brand and technology outward-licensing deals.

His previous experience includes practicing law in the Washington, DC offices of DLA PIPER US LLP and STERNE, KESSLER, GOLDSTEIN & FOX PLLC. Prior to attending law school, he was a software design engineer with GENERAL ELECTRIC and a graduate of the GE Edison Engineering Program.

Mr. Millien is a national lecturer for the BAR/BRI? PATENT BAR REVIEW course, and has served as an adjunct professor of legal writing and oral advocacy at the George Washington University Law School, and a professorial lecturer of IP Law at the George Washington University School of Engineering. He has coauthored the book *Little Blues: How to Build a Culture of Intellectual Property within a Small Technology Company* (Euromoney/MIP, 2006). He has also published several articles, is a frequently-invited speaker, and has been quoted in major national publications and interviewed on local television news.

Mr. Millien received a B.S. from Columbia University, and a J.D. from The George Washington University Law School. He is admitted to the Illinois, New York, Virginia, and District of Columbia bars, and is registered to practice before the U.S. Patent and Trademark Office.

PREFACE TO THE SECOND EDITION

It has been six years since the first edition of From Finals to the Firm was published, and ten years since we delivered our first seminar. While the law continues to evolve, and law practice has changed (or, is changing), the Top 10 we debuted so many years ago are just as relevant today! Thus, we continue to lecture around the country at law schools, bar associations and law firms.

You've taught us a lot along the way. We thank you for your e-mails, questions and illuminating anecdotes. We've taken good notes to improve our ability to help you succeed. In addition, we've spent many hours discussing the Top 10 with senior associates, partners and general counsel from around the country. As a result, we've added new "Sidebars" to many of the original chapters. These Sidebars are written by law firm partners and in-house counsel from around the country, and provide an outside perspective on our tips and offer additional helpful advice. Some of the Sidebars we've written ourselves to provide additional thoughts that expand upon the advice already given in the corresponding Chapter.

The culmination of all of these efforts is this greatly-expanded Second Edition. We hope that a new generation of young lawyers find our insights informative and inspirational. After so many lectures and copies sold, the tremendous positive feedback we've received leaves us with no doubt that following our ten pointers will lead to a more rewarding law firm experience!

Best wishes,

CALVIN GLADNEY
calvin@finalstofirm.com
RAYMOND MILLIEN
raymond@finalstofirm.com

Washington, DC
June 2009

*

PREFACE TO THE FIRST EDITION

About four years ago, we were asked by a national law student organization to deliver a seminar at its national convention. We were given the latitude to choose a topic because we are both former national officers of the organization. Several weeks before the convention date, we met over lunch a few blocks from our respective offices. Our aim for that afternoon was to select the topic and develop the seminar.

Our ultimate goal was to develop and deliver an informative seminar that was relevant to law students preparing to go to law firms, whether as law clerks, summer associates or full-time associates. We wanted a topic that was fresh and not repetitive of any law school class or clinic. That afternoon, "From Finals to the Firm: The Top 10 Things New Law Firm Associates Should Know" was born. We realized that the three-year law school curriculum and bar review lectures did little, if anything, to adequately prepare students for law firm life. We also reflected on our past couple of years of "trial by fire" type learning and thought that our seminar might help students avoid some of the pitfalls awaiting the unwary new associate.

After heartfelt discussions, we developed a list of the top ten lessons we wished we were taught prior to embarking on our law firm careers. A few weeks later, we delivered the seminar to rave reviews. As we suspected, students felt that this information was not (candidly) available anywhere else. The best career development offices at the best law schools did not deliver pointers on the transition from law school to the law firm.

We have since delivered our From Finals to the Firm seminar several times to different audiences around the country. The reaction has been consistently positive. Our status as "younger" attorneys allows us to connect well with students and speak casually, yet informatively. Further, we have discovered through discussions with students who have attended our live seminars that these ten lessons are equally applicable to those going to non-law firm legal jobs as well! It is this overall positive experience that has motivated us to publish this book. Thus, regardless if your goals are to eventually go in-house or make partner, we hope that you find the following pages informative, inspirational and insightful. We have no doubt that following these ten pointers, as we have, will lead to a more rewarding law firm experience and put you well on the way to being the best associate you can be!

Best wishes,

CALVIN GLADNEY
San Francisco, CA
calvin@finalstofirm.com

RAYMOND MILLIEN
Washington, DC
raymond@finalstofirm.com

February 2003

ACKNOWLEDGEMENTS

I would like to thank my mother, Maggie Gladney, for showing me that perseverance and belief in self can overcome any challenge. This book is a reflection of that philosophy.

— Calvin

To Spencer and Katherine

— Raymond

We would like to thank Andrea L. Clay, Jorge A. Goldstein, Shai Littlejohn, Shirin Malkani and DeMaurice F. Smith for their contributions to this Second Edition.

We would also like to thank Ellen Callinan, Adjunct Professor of Law and Library Web Services Coordinator, E.B. Williams Law Library, GEORGETOWN UNIVERSITY LAW CENTER for allowing us to use her "J.U.S.T. A.S.K." research approach which we incorporated into our "Top Ten".

— Calvin & Raymond

*

Table of Contents

*

FROM FINALS TO THE FIRM

THE TOP TEN THINGS NEW ASSOCIATES NEED TO KNOW

Including a Bonus Chapter Exclusively for Summer Associates

EXPANDED SECOND EDITION

*

NO. 1: FIND AN "ANGEL"

You have just graduated from law school and now, with J.D. in hand, you have landed at the firm as a first-year associate. You're bright, eager and (hopefully) confident that you possess all the tools necessary to succeed at the firm. Orientation is over. Computer training is done. Sitting at your desk, you realize that the "recruitment honeymoon" is over. It's lonely in your office and people are no longer knocking on your door everyday volunteering to take you to lunch like when you were a summer associate. It's time to work and earn that salary! What will you do now? How will you succeed at the firm? The answers are neither formulaic nor simplistic. Nevertheless, one of the first things you have to do on the road to success at the firm is find an "angel."

They Don't Wear White and Have Wings

Now, what do we mean by an "angel"? We mean that you need to find a partner (or sometimes, a senior associate) who is going to look out for you and help guide not only your initial acclimation to the firm, but your career as well. Many people often confuse an "angel" with a "mentor." They, however, do not necessarily serve the same function. We are all familiar with mentors. They have guided many of us through high school, college, pre-law school career, law school, etc. These same "life mentors" may continue to serve us by performing their counselor function. We do recognize that you may have gotten this far without a mentor. In the law firm context, however, we do not recommend the "going it alone" approach.

When we speak of an "angel" in the law firm context, we mean someone *within* the firm who will serve to guide you in addition to any outside mentors that you may already have. An angel may serve as your legal mentor, but may also serve you in ways other than mentoring. An angel is someone who knows the "ins and outs" of the firm and can teach you how things work. An angel is someone who is in the position to speak on your behalf and champion your cause during performance and salary reviews, and in practice group or partner meetings. An angel is someone who,

1

when they say good things about you, others will not only listen, but will be influenced as well. An angel is someone who is an "insider" in the position to tell the partnership how talented and bright you are, and about the good work you produce. An angel is someone who can tell you that the senior partner for whom you're currently writing a memorandum hates footnotes. Now you get the picture!

[N.B.: At some firms, other religious-themed terms are used for "Angel," including "Rabbi," "Pastor," and the like.]

Angel Hunting

How do you find an angel? Oftentimes, as luck will have it, an angel will just appear to you. On your first day of work, for example, a partner or senior associate may stop by your office and say: "Hey, how are you doing? My door is always open. Let's do lunch soon." At that point, you should thank your lucky stars because you may have just found your angel rather easily. That is, you'll immediately think to yourself: "This person may be my angel!"

Oftentimes, however, your angel will not just miraculously appear. In such cases, you have to keep your eyes open and observe. Through this process, you need to determine which partners or senior associates have "juice" or "pull" within the firm, are on the right committees or are generally "in the know." It is those people that can give you insight on the inner workings of the firm. It is those people who are going to be at the right meetings and who are going to be able to know what's going on, when the choice assignments are coming up, and where to find the prize assignments. This is not to say that your angel needs to be the firm's chairperson, managing partner or head associate. If so, great! There are plenty of other people, however, who can serve as an angel who do not necessarily hold such titles. So, you should not discount certain potential angels based on titles alone. For example, a senior associate who is regarded by the partnership as the star in your practice group may be an excellent angel despite having no official title.

During the process of finding an angel, it is important not to prematurely disqualify persons who may make the best angels. That is, during the angel identification process, do not restrict yourself to finding someone who went to the same law school or college as you. Similarly, do not restrict yourself to finding an angel who pledged the same fraternity/sorority, played the same intercollegiate sport, comes from the same hometown, practices in the same group, *etc.* Race, gender, religion and the other tribal divisions that humans often adhere to should not be a factor. This is because if you're lucky enough to find an angel, who cares about these silly classifications or superficial divisions!? That person is your angel! Any or all of these perceived differences do not matter. If someone wants to help you and look out for your career, who are you—as a lowly first-year associate—to reject an angel's help?

Upon identifying the above subset of persons at the firm, the choice as to who will be your angel should become apparent. That is, from this subset of persons, you need to perform a further filter and determine who has taken an interest in your career and will be your angel. This entire process, however, may take some time. Do not force the issue and become too aggressive. Also, don't be fake. A true angel will be someone you can bond with and speak with candidly. That is, your angel will become the only person from your firm whom you'll want to invite to a special, private affair—such as your wedding or birthday party—despite the ballooning guest list. In the end, you will not call your angel "angel," nor will your angel necessarily know that he or she is your angel. Rather, you will notice that a mutual respect and admiration among the two of you will develop, along with an easy rapport. This will ultimately result in your angel taking affirmative steps to help your career without being asked.

Beware of the Default Angel

One word of caution is necessary. Many law firms have a "mentor program," "buddy program," or something similarly named. That is, many firms will assign each first-year associate to a partner and/or senior associate for some type of mentoring. These firms will even schedule special mentorship events (e.g., happy hours) or allocate annual mentor-mentee lunch budgets. Don't be fooled by these programs and their pairings. While the partner and/or senior associate assigned to you may eventually turn out to be your angel, don't blindly accept this person as your "default" angel. That partner and/or senior associate may not have volunteered for the assignment and may care little about mentoring a neophyte. By not accepting this default, however, and actively seeking your own angel, you are assured a better fit. In the end, the worst thing that can happen is that you find more than one angel. While we are not divinity experts, we are certain that the more angels you have, the more wonders that can be worked for your career!

In sum, being successful at the firm is not all about how much law you know. Part of the formula is knowing how the game is played at your particular firm and having the right people notice you playing the game well among all the other associates. This is where your angel comes into play. Because, believe it or not, no matter how much law you know, everything you need to succeed at the law firm you didn't learn in law school, or should we say, they didn't teach you in law school. Even if you did learn it or they did teach it to you during law school, there is no guarantee that those lessons hold (particularly or completely) true for the particular firm you now call home for the better part of each day. After reading the remaining chapters of the book (and becoming a *From Finals to the Firm* veteran), you'll be convinced that there was a lot more to learn. Now go find that angel!

SIDEBAR TO NO. 1

By Shirin Malkani, Esq.
B.S. Georgetown University; J.D. New York University
Deputy General Counsel, National Basketball Association, New York

I found my angel before I left law school. After my second year, I worked as a summer associate in the New York office of a large national law firm—Firm X. That summer, I was staffed on an initial public offering (or IPO), where Firm X represented a company planning to go public. Firm Y was representing the underwriters of the offering. The parties convened the transaction's second all-day meeting at the office of Firm X. Following a morning of management presentations and detailed questioning, the clients asked to be left alone "without the lawyers." The attorneys quickly dispersed—the Firm X partner and associate to their offices with the promise to call me when we were reconvening, and the Firm Y partner to the reception area to make a few calls—leaving just me and Billy, a senior associate from Firm Y staffed on the IPO. These were the days before Blackberries, and few associates even had cell phones. He seemed to have nothing pressing to do, no calls to return, no emails to check. My good manners and a vague feeling that I might not want to let another firm's attorney freely roam the halls suggested I invite him back to my office to wait. We chatted amiably for close to an hour before I received the call to return to the conference room.

As an aside, I will note that Firm X had a mentoring program. I arrived that summer with an assigned associate mentor and partner mentor. And my Torts professor had offered the name of her friend, a senior partner at Firm X. I had at least one lunch with each. The associate and partner mentors had been selected because they practiced in areas I had listed among my interests as did my professor's friend. I enjoyed my conversations with each but I felt none of the general ease I had when speaking with Billy. Billy proved to be a better angel than any of the attorneys that the firm or my professor had found because Billy became my friend.

The IPO ultimately did not go forward. Billy gave me his card at our last meeting and suggested I apply to Firm Y to join the incoming associate class the following year. I did and choose to work for Firm Y instead of Firm X following law school. Once I arrived at Firm Y, I understood that Billy had already started his work as my angel. He served on the office's recruiting committee.

He had ensured that I was among the third-year law students invited to call-back interviews following the on-campus recruiting cycle.

I was not staffed on a transaction with Billy until that first winter. I worked those initial months at Firm Y as many first year associates do—without much insight into the people I worked with or the firm I worked for. In the course of our first project together, Billy spoke to me about the preferences of the attorneys I worked for and how to manage clients and their expectations. Partner A appreciated telephone calls versus email but liked no more than one per day with all questions saved for that call. Partner B wanted regular updates and preferred all responses to client questions be sent through her. Client C wanted every response in writing. Billy also identified the staff in the office who made it run well. For example, use the services of the daytime proof reader whenever possible. And Billy supplied me with a map of practice area fiefdoms and the roads of egress. If I wanted to work with Partner C, just go knock on her door.

Perhaps just as important as what Billy told me about others in the firm was that he talked about me to them. I met partners in the hall who seemed to recognize my name and said they hoped to work with me. I found myself warmly greeted by the office manager and legal assistant coordinator—both Billy's good friends and important allies in navigating the office. I heard "through the grapevine" that I did good work.

If you are fortunate enough to make many friends at your firm, you may even find more than one angel. Consider dividing the duties. I made a good friend among the other first-year associates. Leslie worked in the Litigation Department and was the kind of affable and voluble friend every first-year associate should have. In addition to sharing frustrations candidly, we could also share our triumphs. Like Billy, Leslie made sure that her colleagues heard about me and my work. Thanks to her, I found the good reputation Billy had helped create spread into other departments. You might not initially see value in having an angel in another practice area. But when a well-respected litigation partner needs research on a topic in your practice area, perhaps she asks for you. Plus annual evaluations and partnership reviews are often conducted by those outside your department or outside your office. A good reputation throughout the firm can only help you in the future.

So look at the friends you have found at work and consider that more than one may be willing and able to act as your angel. Start with the talkative ones. Those who chat with you, chat with others. These are the people who know what is going on in the office and at the firm. They can identify the "good partners" to work with, the practice areas that are doing well and the staff who can help make your life easier and more productive. Listen to what they say and how they say it. If the talk is all of their own exploits, they may be great friends but not angels. Angels have stories about other people—stories you can learn from and stories from which colleagues can learn about you.

All this is to say that your angel doesn't have to be a senior associate or partner, your angel can also be your friend from work—just one with particular qualities. I will be forever grateful to Billy and Leslie—both of whom are still friends—for what they taught me and what they gave me. Angels indeed.

NO. 2: BE YOUR OWN "ANGEL"

Despite our advice in Chapter 1, the fact is no angel or even outside mentor, friend or relative can help your career more than the person you see in the mirror every morning! At the end of the day, it's still all about you! Being your own angel means being proactive at the firm. You must seek out opportunity and embrace challenge. Being your own angel also means setting goals for yourself and understanding how the angel you find can be of assistance to you. Most of the time, an angel is only as good as what you ask of them. You, and only you, are the Chief Executive Officer (CEO), Chief Financial Officer (CFO) and Chief Technology Officer (CTO) of your career.

Goooooooooal!!!

Just like those boisterous World Cup soccer sportscasters, you should be ecstatic about your team making goals! As your career's CEO, you are the coach of your team (too bad you're also the water boy and the guy who carries the bags as well). As the CEO you are responsible for articulating a vision for your legal career. You must create a blueprint for your time at the firm. When writing your blueprint (and yes, we mean actually writing it down) you should start with longer timeframes and work your way down to goals for shorter timeframes. Even if you ultimately don't put pen to paper, at least think about these goals as we talk about them. Here is the plan:

First, write down an overall three-year goal. What type of lawyer do you plan to be in three years? Don't have a clue? (Don't be discouraged if you're not sure—when Calvin's firm asked him what his interests were as a first-year he wrote down four different areas!) If you're not sure what type of lawyer you plan to be, write down the three firm practice areas that seem to interest you the most. Now that you have some three-year goals, let's break them down a bit further.

Second, write down your goals for your first year. Some of you were probably thinking "Three years at the firm? I'm hoping to make it through three months!'' Don't despair because this next step should be easier: write down your one-year goals. Make a list of the type of projects you want to work on this year in order to achieve your three-year plan. *Your angel can be very helpful in assisting you with setting one-year, project-specific goals.* Analyze each available project and figure out how each project can assist you in your larger goal. There is no chivalry or shame in this game—you must do everything you can to minimize working on assignments that have nothing to do with the type of lawyer you want to be. Ask yourself and your angel: What type of projects can I attempt to work on this year that will give me a greater understanding of the fields of law I'm interested in? Who are the partners and senior associates working on those types of projects? Can my angel hook me up with some of these projects? Which outside organizations will allow me to learn more about the practice of law in my fields of interest? Setting one-year goals will give you a roadmap that will help guide you during the course of the year.

Finally, write down specific goals for the next three months. Firm life flies fast and furious–that casual comment from the partner: "Can you go on Westlaw and figure out the law on prescriptive easements in Virginia and the District of Columbia?'' can turn into a twenty-page memorandum with forty footnotes and a month of time gone! So we think it is best for you to set goals in three-month increments—thus allowing for the inevitable "assignment from hell'' which every new associate will have to endure. Make sure that you set goals that deal with all aspects of doing well—getting good projects, building relationships with a broad group of associates and partners, and becoming involved in at least one outside organization.

"To Bill or Not to Bill?'' That Is the Question.

Regardless of what type of lawyer you want to be, and regardless of whether you're setting three-year, one-year or three-month goals, there is one goal you must always attempt to meet. YOU MUST ALWAYS ATTEMPT TO MEET THE FIRM'S MINIMUM BILLABLE HOURS REQUIREMENT!!! We don't care whether a partner said "It's okay to miss the minimum,'' or whether you heard that another associate missed the minimum and still received a bonus–you are an enlightened *From Finals to the Firm* veteran and know the truth! Firms, with few exceptions, start to rank associates immediately—certain associates become known as rising "stars'' right off the bat, and one surefire way *not* to be tapped as the next Michael Jordan of the firm is to fall below the annual minimum billable hour budget or pace set by the firm. Every firm has a minimum annual billable hours target in mind for associates, although some firms are more rigid and focus on it more than others. *This is true even for firms that say they have no minimum billable hours requirement.* That is, firms that state that they don't have a minimum billable hours requirement really only mean that there isn't a specific, defined amount of hours you have to bill in order to avoid a specific, negative result. For example, if the firm has no defined minimum, you may receive a bonus if you perform well but only bill a relatively low amount of hours. Or, you may be judged relative to the hours billed by other associates in the firm.

Ultimately, firms are tracking and comparing associates as soon as they arrive at the firm. The amount of hours you bill will be a factor in how you are judged as an associate in terms of: (a) How many hours you bill may have an effect on your "status" in your associate class (*i.e.*, are you considered a "star" of your associate class, someone who is doing well but closer to average in the class, or are you an associate who is considered to be trailing behind your class in performance?); (b) Your annual number of hours most likely will be a material consideration in the amount of bonus you receive. Firms must definitively reward associates who work more hours. Giving a hard-working associate a good bonus is one of the ways firms attempt to retain associates despite the droves which leave every year; and (c) The number of hours you bill may affect the type of projects you are assigned at the firm. In addition, if you happen to be in a down legal market or economy your job itself may depend on how many hours you bill!

A partner's or senior associate's natural inclination is to give a "sexy," challenging project to those associates whom they've seen work really hard on their projects and do a good job. In firm life, oftentimes how well you do on the project is directly related to how many hours you put in to get it done! For example, you will turn in a better memorandum or draft a better contract if you take the time to read and revise it more than once. So there will be many instances where working more hours will get you access to better future projects, which in turn will allow you to build your talent, foster the right image and gain needed exposure faster. (More on this in Chapter 3.) Remember, the only reward for good work is more work (and thus, more billable hours)!

Don't Believe the Hype!

In addition, it is not enough to take for granted the firm's stated minimum billable hours requirement! The firm may say 1900 hours a year is the minimum. However, the truth of the matter may be that all associates considered "stars" or "partner-ship material" work at least 2100 hours! Talk to everybody that you can think of to get the real answer. Talk to your angel, talk to your fellow associates, ask trusted partners, and certainly ask anybody you know who has now left the firm. Use this information to set your monthly and yearly billable hours goals, and to decide on projects. (Maybe you need to do that random research assign-ment on Kansas property law just for the billable hours!) Again, you are your own CEO and you cannot afford to miss the *actual* minimum billable hours requirement for any reason.

You cannot afford to miss the minimum as your career's CFO either! Many firms these days are tying bonuses (whether explicitly or clandestinely) largely to the number of hours you bill. Many firms do not give bonuses to those who fail to make the firm's stated annual minimum hours goal. So oftentimes it doesn't make *financial sense* for you to miss the minimum. Some of our fellow associates had a saying: "Never leave money on the table!" If your firm gives out a $10,000 bonus to all associates who hit a minimum of 1800 hours, you made a poor *financial* choice when somehow you only ended up billing 1780 hours last year!

Spend Like There *Is* a Tomorrow!

Being your career's CFO doesn't only encompass worrying about how many hours you bill but how much money you spend! You may decide after your first year (or first month, after that partner calls you into her office for the second time at 4:55 p.m. on a Friday and ruins your weekend), that firm life is not the life for you. Or maybe, in order to work in the practice area you choose, you want to switch from a large firm paying a big salary to a small firm paying less money. Or, maybe you've decided that you really want to be a novelist. (Hey, John Grisham did it, why can't you?)

In 2006, the average graduate had outstanding loans totaling $83,181 for private law school graduates, and $54,509 for public law school graduates. However, despite the eye-popping reports of first-year associate starting salaries of $135,000 to $160,000, this only applied to the small percentage of graduates going to firms with over 500 lawyers. The majority of law school graduates go to firms with less than 10 attorneys and are making a median salary of $40,000 to $45,000 per year.[1]

In addition, you can't always assume that you'll be in control of your destiny. What happens if, heavens forbid, you get voted off the island like most of the contestants on Survivor®? In other words, what if you were laid off from the firm? You may be laid off for no fault of your own (i.e. not because of subpar performance). Suddenly, your monthly income goes from building a nice nest egg in your bank account to "goose eggs" ("goose eggs" is another way of saying lots of zeroes)!!

Given the above-stated financial realities of the legal job market, as your own CFO, you must make wise financial decisions *now* so that you have flexibility when making future career choices. For example, if you plan to stay at the firm for only three years, a failure to make wise financial decisions may force a longer stay because you can't afford to leave. You've heard the stories about the associate making $75,000 to $125,000 a year, but as a third-year associate he has no savings, lives in an apartment and is still bouncing checks. You may also know of someone who has been laid off from the firm, has no near-term job prospects, and has no idea

---

1. *See* Leigh Jones, *About that Huge Salary: It's a Longshot*, National Law Journal Online (July 9, 2007) (*quoting* statistics gathered by the National Association for Law Placement (NALP)).

what they're going to do once their severance runs out (assuming they received a severance!). You are a *From Finals to the Firm* veteran now—you will expect the unexpected!

It's very tempting to work long hours and explain away all of those $20 lunches, $60 dinners and bar crawls where you spend $100 on drinks because, "I work hard and therefore should be able to splurge once in a while." Multiple vacations, rent for a luxury apartment (if possible, save some cash and buy a house with the same mortgage payment as your inflated rent!) and weekend shopping sprees may make you feel better in the short term, but won't mean anything when you're sick and tired of being sick and tired and can't leave the firm because you need that sizeable firm paycheck. Set up an automatic debit out of your direct deposit check that goes to a money market account. Count this money as savings that cannot be touched. Now that you're making good money, pay off those college and law school credit card debts you've been carrying. Keep that old car you've been driving for another year or two. If you're doing those things, you can occasionally splurge without feeling like you're sacrificing your ability to leave the firm (if and) whenever enough becomes enough!

Technology Is Your Friend, Unless It's Your Enemy

Finally, as a new associate, you must also be your own CTO. During your first year at the firm, you must maximize your effectiveness and efficiency, and minimize the cost of using available technology. Okay, tell the truth, you really don't know how to use Westlaw do you? Let us tell you what we mean. During law school, those Westlaw ALLFED (*i.e.*, All Federal Cases) database searches were free and you could take seven hours and a hundred different search term combinations to find that one relevant case and it was no big deal. At the firm, however, the same session may cost the client $2,000 and may cost you the chance to show the partner that you are the most efficient and effective person for that next big assignment. Hey, we admit that when we arrived at our firms we didn't know how to send a "blast fax" (*i.e.*, a simultaneous fax to multiple people at different fax numbers), nor could we tell you how to compare version 2 to version 3 of a document, show the changes made to the old document (this is commonly called "red-lining" or "black-lining" a document) then attach the newest version and the compared version to an e-mail (the compared version is commonly called the "red-lined" or the "black-lined" version), encrypt them and send them over the Internet to a client. Do you? (For all of you technologically-savvy readers who are thinking "I'd just scan it and send it by e-mail as a PDF attachment," what do you do when the scanner is broken or busy?) Some of you are probably reading this and thinking "Actually, I can barely format a document on Microsoft® Word, yet alone add a slide to a PowerPoint® Presentation or create a new record in a Microsoft Access® database!" Your firm, the local bar association and the software licensors themselves may all provide resources for training. If you are unable to get training, just sit down and play around with the program, or ask your secretary for help (more on this in Chapter 4). You can save time, access much needed information quickly, and present a very professional image if you can master the technology offered by the firm. You must also learn as much as you can about all of the free legal resources available on the Internet, and your firm's intranet.

You should now be fully prepared to be your own angel, and to act as the CEO, CFO and CTO of your law firm career. Ultimately, once you finish reading this book, you'll have a better sense of the spectrum of goals you should set for yourself. You will also have a toolkit of savvy tricks of the trade on how to play the law firm game. *From Finals to the Firm* will train you to be your own best angel—just in case you and the angel you find don't agree on what law firm heaven really should be.

Top 8 Ways to Know You Are Not Being Your Own Angel

We hate to end our No. 2 tip of our Top 10 with another list, but—as they say—it is what it is. Thus, we present to you the following eight excuses that Raymond received as a young associate from a partner who had blast emailed them with the admonishment: "If you never have to use these phrases, you most likely will be very successful [here at the firm]."

1. Statement: "It was just a draft."

    (See our advice in Chapter No. 3)

2. Statement: "I did not understand the assignment."

    (See our advice in Chapter No. 5)

3. Statement: "I did not get all the facts."

    (See our advice in Chapter No. 5)

4. Statement: "My plate was too full."

    (See our advice in Chapter No. 4)

5. Statement: "I had never done that before."

    (See our advice in Chapter No. 1)

6. Statement: "It did not show up on Westlaw."

    (See our advice in Chapter No. 2)

7. Statement: "She said she wanted it in a hurry."

    (See our advice in Chapter No. 8)

8. Statement: "I had no idea how long it should take."

    (See our advice in Chapter No. 10)

SIDEBAR TO NO. 2

Andrea L. Clay, Esq.
B.A., UCLA; J.D. and M.B.A., University of Southern California
Partner, Allen Matkins Leck Gamble Mallory & Natsis LLP, San Francisco

Without a doubt, no one can help make or break your career more than you. Partners always appreciate a self-motivated, "go-getter" type of young associate. In promoting yourself, however, don't forget the most basic principle—first and foremost, do good work. Above all else partners want to consistently see (i) high quality work, (ii) completed in a timely manner, (iii) from an associate displaying that "team spirit" and sacrifice for "the team" when needed; and they want to see it all with enthusiasm and a "go getter" attitude. The best way to sell yourself is to sell your ability to consistently perform and the ability to do so under pressure.

Do Good Work in a Timely Manner

Beware of falling into the trap of accepting more projects than you can handle. You may think that there are twenty-four hours in a day, so of course you can finish all the work you have so proudly accumulated for yourself. Because you are a "go getter" and your own angel, you want to show the partners (i) how proactive you are by knocking on their doors and asking for work, and (ii) what a great team player you are by accepting all assignments when asked by partners or senior associates. However, being over-eager can and often does backfire if you accept so many assignments that either (i) you can't reasonably get everything done on time, or (ii) in order to meet the deadlines of each project, the quality of your work suffers. It is far more important to commit to and comply with deadlines while producing high quality work than it is to show the partners how much work you can do at one time. Although partners never want to hear "I am too busy to accept your assignment," they would rather hear this upfront than later hear "I'm sorry, I know the deadline is tomorrow but I haven't gotten to your assignment yet because I'm swamped doing assignments for Partners X, Y and Z," or worse yet have you turn in a rushed project that the partner now has to completely re-do.

Even if you are good at managing the number of assignments you accept, you still can sometimes find that your workload becomes too much if a particular project takes on a life of its own and ends up being far more work than you or the partner originally thought. Be realistic about the workload you can manage, and if you find it gets to an unmanageable level (*i.e.*, there aren't enough hours in the day to get it all done) don't be ashamed to admit it, but be sure you do so early enough in the process for the partner to adjust the timeline with the client or find other associates to help you with the work. An associate who produces high-quality work in a timely manner will always earn higher praise as being dependable and reliable than one who cranks out more projects at a lesser quality or who is routinely late. However, do not read the foregoing to mean that it is better to accept few assignments and leisurely take your time to ensure you produce good work on each one! You also don't want to be known as the associate who does great work but doesn't understand or isn't dedicated to the high demands of firm life (i.e., the associate who isn't willing to sacrifice for the team by putting in the hours needed to get it all done). You have to find the right balance.

Although you may have your own plan as to the type of work you want to do, make yourself available for all types of projects that come your way

While it is important to seek out projects that further your career goals, recognize that in your first couple of years you do not have the luxury of being able to pick and choose your projects. Part of the "team spirit" is accepting whatever work comes your way. You also do not want to become known among the partners as the associate who "cherry picks" projects or worse yet, a young associate who thinks certain work is beneath them. While in your mind this type of attitude is evidence of your focus and commitment to the accelerated development of your career, it is an attitude rarely appreciated by the partners. Every lawyer starts at the bottom. In your first couple of years of practice, you will be the one asked to do the grunt work, and you want to be known as the associate who does so with the same level of enthusiasm you would have for a more complex exciting project. Don't worry, partners always want to snap up the talented associates to work on their deals. If you become known among the partners for reliably producing good work, your years of doing grunt work will be very limited and you will soon have your pick of the projects you really want. Consider grunt work a rite of passage that indeed will pass.

To Bill or Not to Bill, That Is the Question

Notwithstanding whatever altruistic reasons may have led you to choose the law as your profession, the bottom line is most law firms are in the business of making money, not protecting the rights of the weak and the innocent (the bigger the law firm, the more true this becomes), and firms only make money when associates bill hours. Without a doubt, how well you do on a project is directly related to the amount of time you put into it, but always try to make it quality time. While partners want to see you've put in your 2100+ hours (putting smiles on each partner's face at the end of each fiscal year), they don't want to have to write-off or write-down too much of your time because that is perceived as the firm losing money on you. When you accept an assignment, feel free to ask the partner for an estimate of how much time it should take you or if there are any budgetary constraints you should be aware of. If the partner replies "it's a big client and they want us to do everything we can, so money is no object," then bill, bill, bill, but be careful. You don't want to be in the situation where you billed a large number of hours to a project that were either unwarranted given the scope of the project or produced little usable product for the client, because the partner will likely have to write-off some of your time if he/she cannot justify billing the client for it. Important note to all associates: partners *hate* to write-off time. By the same token, do not cheat yourself by not entering all your time. If you legitimately spent the time on the project, enter it and let the partner determine if it needs to be written off. What you may think was excessive time, the partner may think was justified because the partner knows how much time he/she was expecting it would take you, and you may be over or under that figure. Don't short-change yourself on your hours at the end of the year by effectively writing off your own time—it's not your job to decide if the client just got a ton of free work from you!

In summary, as was said before, you are the CEO, CFO and CTO of your own career, and, as with any company, the more you understand the ins and outs of the company, the better you can formulate your plan of attack. Good luck!

NO. 3: T.I.E.

Being successful at the firm involves understanding the necessary components of success and also being willing to take some calculated risks. It is difficult to take risks, however, until you understand which building blocks must be put into place in order for the risks you take to translate into successes. In this chapter we present three such building blocks using the acronym "T.I.E." Calvin first heard of this handy acronym at a seminar offered by a business-oriented summer internship program he attended during college. We thought it so useful that we now apply it to the law firm environment. This is yet another useful tool for your expanding "Associate Toolkit."

Three Components for Success

It is easy to get caught in a trap at the firm where you spend all of your time trying to build your talent—*i.e.*, becoming the best darn lawyer the firm has ever seen. But which associates get the best assignments is not only determined by who is the most talented. Talent isn't everything. You already know this! Remember the student in Criminal Law who everyone thought was so smart during the first semester because she was so articulate in class ... until you later found out she got a C+ on the final!? Initially, that was "image" at work! Do you remember the student who was chosen to be Student Bar Association president—it wasn't because he was the best candidate, rather it was because everybody knew him! That was "exposure" at work!

You, being the *From Finals to the Firm* veteran that you are, will no longer fall for the old "smoke and mirrors" trick. You understand that success at the firm will involve obtaining top notch legal skills (*i.e.*, Talent), building a persona and reputation as a person who is smart, hardworking and eager to learn and get things done (*i.e.*, Image) and also making sure that the people important to fulfilling the goals you set in Chapter 2 know who you are and how talented you are (*i.e.*, Exposure). An acronym for remembering these three components of success—talent, image and exposure—is

T.I.E. In order to be successful at the firm you must make sure that you are focusing on all three of these factors.

Talent

First, focus on the "talent" component by obtaining assignments that teach you the fundamentals of lawyering in your desired practice area. There is no substitute for learning by fire. Supplement this work by reading articles or trade publications in your field so that you are familiar with the latest cases, practice methods or challenges. Find out (from your angel or senior associates) which journals, magazines, advance sheets, etc. the attorneys in your practice area often read. You want to read publications that will help you be a better lawyer in your field because they give you practical tips, and keep you up-to-date while being relatively quick reads. You will need to make the time (*e.g.*, every Sunday) to get this reading done. Think of it as part of your job.

Image

Perfecting your "image" is just as important as building your talent. It doesn't matter how well versed you are in the latest ways to draft a motion to dismiss if all the top litigators at the firm believe that you are lazy and not thorough when it comes to researching cases. Building a top-notch image is also not a function of appearance alone. (Hey, don't get us wrong. It can definitely help if you look like Brad Pitt or Halle Berry, but good looks alone won't write a brief or draft a sale agreement!) You do need to dress like a professional and understand your firm's stated and unstated dress code. (Notice we advise that you need to "understand" your firm's dress code, not "conform"—we'll talk more about that a little later.)

Building the right image, however, does not stop at your choice of Brooks Brothers over The Gap for work clothing. Image building also involves being articulate and knowledgeable when asked a question (or smart enough to say "I don't know, but I'll get back to you."). It also involves being seen as a team player, a hard worker and someone who can be trusted to get the job done efficiently and effectively. In firm life, young associates get big points for stepping up to take on additional tasks without prodding and working long hours to the benefit of the client.

The right image also involves your demeanor as you walk around the office. After many a late night, or after months working on a project or in a department you have no interest in, it can be difficult to look enthusiastic and smile as you pass your colleagues in the hallways of the firm. In fact, you may honestly think that your life sucks! Yet, looking enthusiastic, smiling and not to mention, being well-groomed (*i.e.*, showered, shaved and neatly dressed), is exactly what you need to do. As a law firm consultant once put it: "Partners hate their lives. They're overworked and stressed out and slaves to the billable hour."[2] Thus, you don't want to be the young associate that acts as a mirror for the partners of your firm and reminds them of how they feel every time they see you in the hallway!

In all areas of the law, one of the key work products attorneys produce is documents. Going the extra mile to make sure that a document (*e.g.*, a memorandum, contract, brief, etc.) is well done is crucial. *A good tip: Have a trusted friend who is a more senior associate, your angel at the firm or outside mentor give a quick read of your first major brief, memorandum or document before you submit it to your supervisor.* (We say this keeping in mind, of course, that you must be careful not to reveal client confidences and inadvertently waive any attorney-client privilege.) Invariably, they will find mistakes or omissions that can significantly affect your image to the client, partner or senior associate receiving the document. Remember, there is no such thing as turning in a "first draft"!

In addition, find examples on your firm's computer document management system of similar documents drafted by your supervisor or your supervisor's favorite associates (and ask other associates for examples too!). Use these documents as a guide to the style, structure and substance that is required by your supervisor. No need to be coy about it. As you find examples in the beginning, ask your supervisor whether the document you found is a good model. Unfortunately, human nature at firms sometimes will cause a rookie mistake or an initial bad impression to brand you negatively on a long-term basis. Any steps you can take to avoid a major mistake are well worth the extra time. In your first year, always put a newly-drafted document to the side, do something else and then read it again later. All lawyers, young and old, will make mistakes. However, the key is to avoid making too many major ones early in your career. The resulting negative image may prevent you from being able to showcase your talents in the future.

Exposure

Being a great talent with an exceptional image means nothing if only you and your secretary know it to be true. Without exposure, your talents can go unnoticed and consequently, unappreciated and untapped. Here's how you should think about this: You want to be somewhere between the peacock who struts its bright feathers for the world to see and the ostrich who has his head buried in the sand. In other words, you want to be aggressive about exposure but

2. Ashby Jones, *The Third Year Dilemma: Why Firms Lose Associates*, The Wall Street Journal (Jan. 4, 2006).

not "over the top." Exposure means getting staffed on the projects that are important to the firm, or are important to important clients of the firm, or are important to the important people in the firm. But getting placed on those projects is only half of the battle. You want to do well on those projects. As a new associate you want exposure to as many people, resources and practice areas as possible—it's amazing how a miscellaneous research project on something you didn't think you were interested in can turn into your area of specialty!

You can get exposure in a variety of ways. Getting exposure may simply require going up to the partners who do the work you want to do and indicating your interest in working with them on future projects. You can also use your angel to get exposure. Remember how we told you in Chapter 2 that the best angel is only as good as what you ask of them? You can ask your angel to put in the good word for you with the partners and senior associates you want to work with on desired projects. In addition, your angel can tell you which firm committees or non-billable projects might help you get the word out on your talent or to build a positive image. Your angel can also warn you about the associates and partners you don't want to work with because they will suck you in and never let you back out!

Braids, Beards and Belief in Self

Now that you understand how to cultivate your talents, build your image and get exposure, let's discuss what you should do when you might want to take some risks with respect to image. The question we address here is: "What do you do when you want to present an image that doesn't conform to the 'norms' of your firm?" Here are a couple of examples:

You are a male third-year law student and usually wear your dyed blonde hair somewhat spiked. You also sport a small diamond stud in your ear. You're about to go on an interview for an associate position at a firm. Should you ditch the earring and mellow out your hair to give a more "conservative" appearance?

You are an African–American woman and wear your hair in braids. You didn't have braids during your interview, but after taking the bar and summer vacation, you do now. Just before your first day at the firm you're thinking about whether to leave in the braids. Should you take out the braids before starting at the firm?

You are a male, second-year law student and wear a full beard. Facial hair, including mustaches, is not common at the firm you're interested in working for. Should you cut off your facial hair before going on an interview?

Each of the above examples presents a situation for performing a risk/benefit analysis. They also require an analysis of what's most important to you. Lastly, it's a question of picking battles and knowing which wars you can't win. Notice we didn't name this section "Eyebrow Piercings, Facial Tattoos and Taking on the Establishment!" This is because at an overwhelming majority of firms, those are battles you are simply *not* going to win!

Your decisions on appearance are personal ones and a personal analysis will guide you to an answer. First, decide how important the item in question is to you. Is it cultural, religious, or just a matter of personal style? Do you feel that you are giving up an essential part of yourself if you conform? Will you never forgive yourself? Can you conform for the interview but change back once you get to the firm? Can you come up with a middle ground with which you're comfortable (*e.g.*, would it work for you to shave your beard, but keep your mustache?). Second, analyze the possible ramifications of making the move you're considering. What's the worst thing that can happen and how has this issue played out previously at the firm? Your angel, friends and law school career counselor can be helpful in thinking about the risks and giving you a historical and objective perspective. Will you be hired? Will you be fired? Shunned from the high profile or coveted projects? Is the firm progressive and casual, or conservative and rigid? Where are the firm's clients along that spectrum?

Lastly, don't let a short-term fashion statement become a long-term image issue! For example, tattoos are really in vogue right now. But ladies, do you really want that butterfly tattoo you're thinking about getting on your left shoulder blade to be visible under your strapless black dress at the firm black-tie dinner? Gentlemen, do you really want that barbed wire chain which goes around your right bicep to be seen at the firm's annual golf outing? If you're going to get a tattoo, get one in a place that will be inconspicuous when you need it to be. After reading this chapter, you know that you must build your talent, solidify your image and get lots of positive exposure. Oftentimes, you'll notice more senior or very well respected associates and partners bucking conformity more than others.

One method for taking risk is to establish yourself as a talented associate first, get the lay of the land and then make a reasoned decision on a course of action with regard to any "non-conforming" appearance issues. Who knows, maybe six months later you don't want to wear the earring anymore or maybe you're tired of braids! Whatever your appearance, taking risks which distinguish you from the "mainstream" should be calculated. It also requires you to do more, because successful new associates are not complacent about increasing their talents, fostering the right image or gaining necessary exposure.

SIDEBAR TO NO. 3

Shai Littlejohn, Esq.
B.A. and J.D. Howard University
General Counsel, DC Sports and Entertainment Commission, Washington, DC

Talent, image, and exposure—T.I.E.—all contribute to brand YOU. Think of yourself as a branded product. To sell yourself, you must convince partners that you provide a useful service. The interview merely provided a quick advertisement of who you are and what you claim you can offer. If you already work for a firm, then you passed the first test. The firm made a rather impulsive buy based on what attributes you appeared to possess and how well its partners reasoned you would perform. The advertisement was good enough to land you the job, but once you arrived in a neatly presented package, did buyer's remorse set in because whatever was on the inside of the package failed to meet expectations?

Talent

Talent is part of brand YOU, and brand YOU is what makes or breaks your career. Talent is the "T" in the T.I.E. that partners and senior attorneys consider when determining your usefulness. Talent is simply the skills and abilities that make you useful.

One of the best kept secrets is that your talent is never just about you. In law school, your efforts and grades were, in fact, all about you. You decided when to study, and you alone owned your grades. However, in the work force and particularly early in your career, you are there to help others perform. When your talent makes the partner look good, then you are on the way to becoming essential simply because you are useful. As long as you help the partner perform better, and make his or her job easier, then you fill an essential role. However, if you fail to demonstrate how you are needed, partners might decide that you are no longer. Consider what substantive contributions you can offer to make the partner more effective in his or her job. *Effective display of talent includes intelligence, thoughtfulness, diligence, accuracy, and interest in the chosen practice area.* Talented attorneys perform the desired tasks no matter what the pressure or circumstance, and as a result, they take the load off of others. When a partner or senior attorney gives a project to you, assure them that with you, it will be done.

Image

Image is the second component of brand YOU. Which words would partners use to objectively convey your approach to work: resourceful, goal-oriented, energetic, intellectual, dedicated, timely and reliable; or complacent, late, difficult, overly-confident, sensitive, unreliable and inconsistent? Do your colleagues respect you, or do they consider you an opportunity hog, overly competitive, and untrustworthy? The image that you present is part of brand YOU.

All you've got is your reputation. Your reputation is the image that others have of you, and once you begin to establish a negative image, it is difficult to reverse. People judge closely your behavior in stressful or adversarial situations. If you make a mistake, quickly take responsibility. Be honest and ethical at all times. Make ethical decisions regarding your conduct inside and outside of the workplace.

Exposure

Once you cultivate talent, and present a positive brand image, you are ready for exposure. Exposure is the final and indispensable component of brand YOU. Exposure gives you confidence, and confidence paves the way for better assignments. Sitting secluded in an office for ten hours per day is not exposure. Making time for lunch or a cup of coffee with a senior associate or mingling through a firm reception, however, is exposure. Running straight home after work is not exposure, taking an evening or two each week to engage in neighborhood civic associations or work on political campaigns is exposure. Exposure to different people and issues breeds depth of character and a well-rounded perspective. As you engage in conversations with partners and associates, they are listening for signs of exposure. They are watching *for similarities in values and experiences.* People want to be around like-minded folks. The similarities or lack thereof, are part of your brand image.

When you employ T.I.E., you are better able to believe in and sell brand YOU. You can take pride in knowing that your product is valuable because it is useful. You have not feigned your way through; rather, you earned your stripes. So be true to you. Pursue the practice areas, topics and positions that you are most interested in, regardless of salary or perception of prestige. If firm life is too uncomfortable, ask yourself: "Is this where I really want to be?" If the answer is "no," then start working your way to where you do want to be. Lawyers who correctly employ T.I.E. have options. If and when you discover that firm life is not for you, you can capitalize on the talent, image, and exposure that is brand YOU and move on to other opportunities.

Remember, you are a marketing executive creating a branded product. You want to convince buyers that you are responsive, timely, committed, capable and smart. Brand YOU is consistent. Partners know what they are going to receive from working with you. Convince them that you are the product that they need. Show them that you invest in yourself and others. Eventually, one is likely to invest in you.

SIDEBAR TO THE NO. 3 SIDEBAR

You probably read the heading and said to yourself "Can there really be a sidebar to a sidebar?" Well, we did name Chapter 7 "Think Outside The Box"—we're just taking our own advice!

In Chapter 3—"T.I.E."—you learned that fostering the right image and getting great exposure were as critical as building your legal talent. Shai Littlejohn expanded on this concept in her Sidebar—noting that "talent, image and exposure—T.I.E.—all contribute to brand YOU." Well, we write this sidebar *deux* to remind you that brand YOU should be carefully built not only in the real world (*e.g.*, at the firm happy hour or at the bar association mixer) but also in that Wild Wild West known as the Internet.

Do you have a Facebook® or a MySpace® page? Do you have a personal blog? Are you connected to people on LinkedIn®? Do you Twitter®? If you answered "yes" to any of these questions now ask yourself the following: Are you fostering the right Image, getting the right Exposure and properly showcasing your Talent on these online venues?

Now you might be saying to yourself that you already have the job, that's why you're reading this book, and so you don't need to worry about some interviewer checking out those law school pictures you buried on your Facebook® page. But, have you "Googled" yourself lately? When you get assigned to a new matter, and the client says "Who is this new associate?" and decides to let the Web tell your story, what story will be told? Will it jive with the image you're fostering with your colleagues and superiors?

Let us also let you in on a little secret: Nearly 80% of all associates leave their firm by the end of five years.[3] Thus, you're eventually going to be a job-seeker again. You'll be a job-seeker with an extensive virtual brand YOU comprised of every salacious picture, off-color comment and inappropriate association you've ever allowed to be documented online.

So be smart about what you put online for the world (literally!) to see. We told you in Chapter 2 that you need to be your own CEO, CFO, and CTO. Well make some additional room on your career business card because you need to be your own CMO (Chief Marketing Officer) as well! To that end, here are a couple bits of advice:

    1) *Take down inappropriate pictures.* Even if you have been "paling around with terrorists" does the world have to have

---

3. Elizabeth Goldberg, *Moving On Inevitable for Many Midlevels*, National Law Journal Online (Aug. 17, 2006) (*quoting* statistics gathered by NALP).

the pictures to prove it? You want to absolutely control your colleagues' and supervisors' visual impression of you. One forwarded e-mail and your co-workers may never look at you the same—this will without a doubt affect your reputation at the firm.

2) *Have a relatively apolitical web presence.* Right or wrong, the color of the firm's political party is often green, rather than red or blue. Federal campaign donations are usually available as a public record online, but extensive diatribes on the idiocy of the party you don't support are voluntary on your part. We should be clear—many firms and their partners have political leanings—but as you're doing your best to fit into the firm and become a star, there is no need to turn off the partnership or a potential angel before you show them your unquestionable talent.

3) *Proofread all public profiles.* A young man reached out to Calvin the other day by e-mail for a job. Calvin promptly went on his LinkedIn page and it was replete with spelling and grammatical errors. Guess who has an uphill battle to prove that he's meticulous enough to work with Calvin?

4) *With Friends Like These* ... So you follow our advice, clean up your Web act and feel that all is well in the world. But then one day you realize that one of your good friends has been blogging incessantly about that time that you and she ... Make sure that you get your friends to follow numbers 1 and 2 above with respect to your virtual presence as well.

5) *Be Proactive. Brand YOU should be your own creation.* There are a number of websites that allow you to network with thousands of like-minded future colleagues, bosses or business partners. Keep your public profiles up-to-date and let people know the wonderful new projects you've completed. Let them know the organizations with which you're working. You never know who's surfing and looking for a talented *From Finals to the Firm* veteran like you!

NO. 4: THE STAFF IS IT!

Alphabet Soup and Arrogance

You have a B.A. or a B.S. You may have an M.A., M.S. or M.B.A. You may even have a Ph.D. This is in addition to your J.D. Now, you may arrive at the firm and find out that your assigned secretary has only a G.E.D. That fact, however, does not make you B.E.T.T.E.R. than your secretary! Don't be arrogant and think you know more than your secretary because you have an alphabet soup behind your name. You don't! This is because, chances are, when it comes to the *mechanics* of practicing law, your secretary simply knows more than you! (When Raymond started as a first-year associate, for example, his secretary had over eight years of patent experience! Who do you think was telling whom what to do?)

Have you ever filed a patent application? Do you know what forms need to be filed and how they should be formatted? Have you ever filed a complaint at the local federal district court? Do you know what a Civil Cover Sheet is or what it should look like? Have you ever filed a registration statement with the SEC and do you know what its format should be? Chances are you haven't done any of these things. Being your own angel, however, demands that you do *not* become an expert in these mechanics. You want to devote the majority of your energy and brainpower to the *substantive* practice of law. In order to be successful and completely and competently represent clients, however, these mechanical aspects of practicing law must be done correctly.

You have successfully gotten through your law school curriculum, but you probably have not taken a personnel management class. Even as a first-year associate, however, it is your job to "manage" the firm's staff as part of serving clients' needs. Now, by "manage" we do not mean "boss around." Rather, we mean that the staff is an asset that you must use effectively. Further, when we use the term "staff" in our advice that "the staff is it," we mean not only your secretary, but also the paralegals, the kitchen and host staff that set up the conference rooms, and the mailroom, copy center, word processing department and library personnel.

It is up to you to think of and manage the firm's staff as a valuable resource for being successful in the practice of law at the firm. How do you treat the staff in a way that makes them feel like a valuable part of the team? Well, many of the things you need to know, you learned in kindergarten: say "please," say "thank you," and just be nice. These are basic courtesies that (we hope) should go without saying. The remaining things you need to know include remembering to always give clear instructions and to give as much advance notice as possible to allow staff to accurately complete tasks that you've assigned to them.

It is your job to inspire your secretary (and the rest of the staff) to work for you. How do you do that? Well, as they say in the pop culture, "don't trip!" Here's an example. Instead of barking orders at staff such as: "Type this!", "Mail that!", or "Copy this!", take an extra minute or two to explain the big picture. That is, explain the overall project and how important it is to the client that it be completed by the stated deadline. When people understand their role as part of a team, rather than feeling that they are only being given menial and disjointed tasks, they're more inspired to perform.

In return for doing the above, you'll be amazed at the treatment you receive. Your faxes will arrive on your desk before the ink dries, your photocopies will be handed to you while the paper is still warm, important overnight packages will come up from the mail room first thing in the morning, the treatise the library did not have will land on your desk the next morning courtesy of an inter-library loan, and the reimbursement for that $1,000 travel expense charged to your personal credit card will arrive from accounting without the normal two-week delay. Understand now? Further, the sooner the staff completes tasks you've assigned them, the sooner you can complete projects assigned to you by the partners.

What Is Efficiency?

In a number of firms, one of the key metrics partners use to measure associates is called "efficiency." For example, if you bill five hours for a project that the partner responsible for preparing that client's bills thinks should have taken only three hours, the partner may only charge the client for those three hours (*i.e.*, she will "write off" the extra two hours you billed). Thus, for that project, your efficiency was only 60% (*i.e.*, three hours actually *billed* to the client divided by the five *billable* hours spent). Taking this metric a bit further, efficiency can be calculated for each associate over the course of a fiscal quarter and eventually over the course of a fiscal year for all projects worked on for that time period. Consequently, the more efficient you are, the more valuable you become to clients and the more revenue you generate for the firm. (At some firms, your efficiency will in some way be reflected in your annual bonus and/or raise.)

Why did we just explain efficiency and its calculation? Well, it was not to bore you with useless math. Rather, in the above example, did you spend part of those extra two hours that were "written off" making edits to a document that could have been done by your secretary? Did you spend part of those extra two hours standing over the fax machine instead of giving it to someone in the mailroom to send for you? Did you spend part of those extra two hours photocopying cases rather than having a paralegal or someone from the library do it for you? (*Caution*: Never cut your own time! Let the partner—because it's her client—decide how many of those five hours to actually bill out. It may just be that she and the client think it should have taken ten hours!)

One more example. Let's say a partner hands you an eight-inch stack of documents one afternoon and tells you: "The CEO and CFO of XYZ.com are coming tomorrow morning at 8:30 to join us for breakfast and want to discuss these SEC documents. Can you grab a conference room?" Naturally, of course, all you say is, "Yes." Now, a conference room needs to be reserved, breakfast needs to be ordered and set up for delivery, copies of the documents need to be made and placed in the conference room before 8:30 a.m., and not to mention, you have to read the documents in order to prepare for the meeting. These tasks need to get done in addition to a memorandum you were finishing for another partner. Do you want to spend your time coordinating bagels, coffee and copies? Do you have such time? The answer is obviously "no." Do you think the partner will coordinate them? Don't be ridiculous! If the clients arrive that next morning and there is no breakfast, coffee, four place settings of silverware and four clean copies of the documents, who will the partner think is not dependable? You! So, what do you do? Well, the staff is it! You need to call your secretary and manage the various staff to coordinate all of these "meeting logistics." This leaves you free to concentrate on preparing for the meeting by digesting that eight-inch stack of documents.

The lesson to be learned by all of the above examples is that you want to devote as much of your time as possible to the substantive practice of law. The goal is to complete tasks for clients in the smallest amount of billable hours possible (*i.e.*, being efficient). Therefore, you do not want to spend billable hours sending faxes, sending overnight letters, making copies, ordering food, making reservations, or otherwise performing tasks that are better handled by staff. (Obviously, there are some pinch situations (*e.g.*, after-hours, weekends, *etc.*), where you will not only have to perform such tasks, but you will need to know *how* to perform such tasks as part of being your own angel.)

Added Benefits

Treating and managing the staff well will not only help you be more efficient (and not to mention, is part of being a good human being), but it has other advantages as well. First, some law firms have begun evaluating how well associates manage and relate to their secretaries and other staff as part of (salary and bonus) performance reviews. Thus, you have a financial incentive, as the CFO of your career, to manage the staff appropriately.

Second, treating certain staff well will result in access to information not generally available. For example, let's consider the secretaries who work for the partners and senior associates for whom you do work. That is, many partners and senior associates have mastered the concept of "the staff is it." So it's not surprising that such partners and senior associates trust their secretaries— many of whom have been with them for ten or more years—more than any other person at the firm. Consequently, their secretaries may know the most about what's really going on with certain projects or even within the firm as a whole. If you build a genuine and positive relationship with these secretaries, you'll be surprised how much of a good word they can put in for you, how they'll make sure you can get on their attorneys' busy calendars, and how they can give you feedback on work you've done for these attorneys who oftentimes are too busy to remember to give you such feedback directly.

Even if you don't have the opportunity to interact with partners' (or senior associates') secretaries for whom you do work, don't be surprised when you find out that many of them often have lunch with *your* secretary. That is, beware that the staff at most firms are a tight-knit community! So, if you're rude to one (or two) of them, word will get around, a negative reputation about you will spread, and the services that you require to be successful at the firm may somehow escape you. If you don't believe us, try offending or upsetting a partner's secretary, and see how well that eventually endears you to the rest of the staff (and not to mention, how well that immediately endears you to that partner). Or, trust us, and just know that *"**the staff is it!**"* "It" being a key part to your success at the firm.

SIDEBAR TO NO. 4

To further illustrate "the staff is it," allow us to share a story told to us by one of our law school seminar attendees. She had recently accepted a summer associate position with a major Wall Street firm after her second year. She was given a nice office which included a desk lamp. Well, she soon discovered the lamp's light bulb was blown out. Thus, she decided to go down to the firm's supply room to find a replacement bulb. She quickly located where the bulbs were located within the supply room—bottom shelf, right by the door. She then bent down (nice suit and all) to find the right sized bulb with the right wattage. As she was on her knees, reaching for the back of the bottom shelf, a senior partner who was on the summer associate committee was walking down the hall and noticed her.

"What are you doing?" he asked.

"Looking for a new light bulb for the lamp in my office," she replied.

"We don't pay you to change light bulbs," the partner replied as he shook his head and walked away.

The Staff Is It!

NO. 5: J.U.S.T. A.S.K.

A Hypothetical

It's 5 p.m. and you just received a phone call. It's one of the partners, and she's in a hurry and has a research assignment for you. You rush down to her office with pen and notepad in hand. As you arrive at her office, she's dictating changes to a document to another associate, her cell phone is ringing and her packed luggage sits next to her desk. She motions you to sit in one of her visitor's chairs.

"I want you to research the law on easements by necessity for my client, New York Corporation. I think there may be something about that in the A.L.R. Figure out whether those easements 'run with the land.' Focus on that question, but keep in the back of your mind as you research that we may have to settle for just a usufruct."

She then thinks for a second.

"Put your answer in a short memo and fax it to my hotel in New York City. I need the answer by 7 a.m. tomorrow so I can review it in time for my 9 a.m. meeting with New York Corporation. Got it? Thanks."

You dutifully grab your notepad and scurry back to your office. You are now sitting down at your desk when a barrage of questions starts swirling in your head: New York Corporation has properties in five states, including New York . . . does she want me to research the law in all five states? Just in New York State? In some other state? What did she mean by "A.L.R."? The librarian has gone home, so I can't ask him for help! You vaguely remember from first-year law school property class what it means for something to "run with the land," but the real question is: What in the world is a "usufruct"? As a matter of fact, do you really know that you've spelt "usufruct" correctly!?

The above hypothetical highlights another golden rule that, as a *From Finals to the Firm* veteran, you should know and will always remember: *The best chance to understand a project is at the beginning!!!* You want to clearly understand the assignment to avoid wasting time and money. That is, if you and your supervisor are not on the same page, you will have to go back and perform the correct research and rewrite the memorandum. Who will pay for that? It will either be, at your supervisor's discretion, you (in terms of written-off hours that negatively affect your efficiency) or the client (in the form of a higher legal tab).

In the above hypothetical, your lack of understanding is partially the supervisor's fault because of her hurried, unclear instructions. At the end of the day, however, it is you who will take the heat if the fax doesn't show up on time the next morning. Thus, we now share with you a tool that we discovered helps younger associates better understand all facets of research projects when they are first assigned. The tool is an approach that follows the acronym: "J.U.S.T. A.S.K."

Let's use the above hypothetical as framework to dissect each component of the acronym. We advise that you write "J.U.S.T. A.S.K." in the margin of your notepad every time you first meet a supervisor who is giving you a research assignment. The acronym will help you recognize the important information in the conversation with the supervisor and also help generate clarifying questions to ask the supervisor before you walk out of her office. At the end of this chapter, after we dissect the acronym, we've included a one-page chart summarizing the approach for your future use.

J = Jurisdiction

The supervisor was not clear as to which jurisdiction she wanted you to research. She didn't specify whether it was one specific state, multiple states, a federal circuit that encompasses a certain state or jurisdiction, or whether she just wanted to know the conclusions and insights garnered from the "seminal" or most significant cases, regardless of the state or jurisdiction. Finding out which jurisdiction to focus on is critical to focusing your research. Researching and writing a memorandum on irrelevant law is not a steppingstone to becoming a "superstar" associate. Thus, you should never walk out of the supervisor's office without knowing that piece of information. (Even if you know an issue is a federal one, a specific circuit's or district court's law may be of most interest to the supervisor.)

U = Useful Tips

Luckily, your supervisor gave you a useful tip—she mentioned that there may be something in the A.L.R. about the research topic. (We'll explain the "A.L.R." in the Acronym section below.) Always ask the supervisor whether they are aware of any articles or other documents written on the topic, or whether there are any firm attorneys who could be a key source of information (*i.e.*, an internal "expert"). Who knows, there may be a recent article that references all of the latest case law in the relevant jurisdiction. You will never know to look for it if you don't ask. In addition, ask the supervisor whether there have been any previous internal memoranda written on the topic. The author of the internal memorandum or the memorandum itself may be a valuable resource for the answer to your question. You may also want to quickly scan the firm's internal document management system to see if a previous memorandum on the topic exists. (As your career's CTO, make sure you learn how to efficiently search the firm's document management system for relevant documents.)

S = Scope

It is critical for you as the associate to understand how extensively your supervisor wants you to research and to understand the exact type of work product that should result from your research. For example, in the above hypothetical, does the supervisor want an eight-page memorandum on the topic, or does she only want a quick overview that summarizes court decisions on the issue without a comparison of the facts? How many hours does the supervisor want you to spend researching and writing the memorandum? Should you research and discuss only current case law? Should you cite secondary sources like law review articles and periodicals? Should you look for and include any pending legislative actions that may affect that law? The answers to all of these questions are important because they will give you a sense of how much time you need to get the job done well. Therefore, you must ask your supervisor these questions to help you understand exactly what the supervisor's expectations are for the work product you will eventually submit to her.

T = Terms of Art

When the supervisor noted that a "usufruct" might be an alternate option, you immediately should have asked for the meaning of that term. *Do not be afraid to ask questions when first receiving an assignment.* This includes questions to which you believe the supervisor thinks you should already know the answer. A supervisor will always prefer you to ask a "stupid" question now, rather than spend precious billable hours trying to answer it on your own. In reality, as you've often heard, the only "stupid" questions are those that go unasked. So ask about any terms of art thrown at you by unfocused supervisors. Oftentimes, the supervisor—who has been practicing for years—does not realize that they are using terms of art no longer used in law school (or were never used in law school) and thus, may be unfamiliar to a new attorney. Further, the definition of every term of art cannot be found in your legal dictionary! Some of you are thinking "Dude, I'd just Google®

it or find it on Wikipedia®!'' Well, you don't always find accurate information on the Web. Secondly, you may not find a definition that fits the context in which you're working.

Lastly, when researching an area of the law you are unfamiliar with, ask the supervisor: "Are there any terms of art that may be useful when doing my research?" This is important because it is often difficult to find the relevant cases using a legal encyclopedia or treatise, or even formulating a Westlaw term search, if you don't know the right terms of art for that specific area of the law.

A = Acronyms

It is difficult to research an issue if you do not know the meaning of an acronym. Yet, more experienced attorneys frequently employ acronyms and assume that everyone (including newer attorneys) knows their meaning. If you don't know the meaning (or even the correct spelling) of an acronym, however, just ask the supervisor. It is much easier and efficient to ask, than to spend hours trying to determine an acronym's meaning on your own. In the hypothetical above, you want to avoid walking around the library aimlessly, without the aid of a librarian, trying to find the "A.L.R." (*i.e., the American Law Reports*, in case you forgot from your first-year Legal Research and Writing class), without first knowing what the acronym means (*i.e.*, knowing the full name of the source you've been directed to search).

S = Sources

As a new associate, you want to be as efficient as possible in researching and writing a memorandum (preferably, citing primary authority). One way to increase your efficiency is to search and use the least amount of sources as possible. Who knows, maybe there is a treatise called *Gladney & Millien on Easements* that will lead you directly to all of the latest case law. Because they have years of experience and have actually used such sources to do their own research, always ask supervisors for the names of any Web sites or secondary sources such as treatises, periodicals, loose-leaf services, Restatements, hornbooks and the like that may speed up your research and help you quickly find out the answer to the question being researched.

K = Key Cost Constraints

As we discuss in more detail in Chapter 10, it is important to understand the cost constraints applicable to your client (in general) and the specific matter to which your current research assignment relates. If your client (or the supervisor) has decided to only allocate a few hours to finding the answer to your research question, you know that you cannot do an exhaustive search and reading of the case law before drafting a memorandum. The client may be unwilling to pay for the cost associated with an associate researching on Westlaw, and thus you may have to rely on free sources available on the Internet. Alternatively, the client may want to forward the firm's memorandum on a critical issue directly to its Board of Directors, and thus may not care about computer research-related costs. Your supervisor will know the cost constraints that affect your assignment, but may forget to mention them to you. Therefore, it is your job to ask! In response, the supervisor may tell you "let's not spend too much on this," or "don't worry about costs, just get it done on time!"

One word of caution: Regardless of cost constraints, never cut corners by failing to check the pocket parts while performing your research and Shepardize cites to all primary authority you rely on in your memorandum.

Update, Update and Update!

A common mistake made by new associates is to expend a significant number of hours on a research project without consulting with the supervisor as to whether the work done so far meets their expectations. For example, you should always go back to a supervisor and update them on your progress on a large research assignment, just to make sure that you are on the right track. The supervisor may decide that it is not worth it to continue doing additional research. The supervisor, after hearing which cases you've found, may decide to brief the client verbally and that she doesn't want you to write a memorandum after all. Or, she might decide that the issue is more complicated than even she first thought, and authorize you to do a more extensive memorandum than she originally requested. Ultimately, you want to "check in" with the supervisor in the middle of a long assignment to better ensure that your current progress meets their expectations and that you are clear as to what should be your final work product.

In order to update your supervisor, a formal meeting with a first draft of your memorandum as the point of discussion is not always necessary. You may simply give the supervisor a call or send her an e-mail with an update on your success in finding relevant case law, along with your thoughts on how much more time it will take to finish the assignment and a request to confirm the desired final work product. You can also ask them questions that may have arisen during your research. Another way to get interim feedback is to draft an outline of your memorandum that includes the main topics, cases and conclusions you intend to discuss.

The J.U.S.T. A.S.K. approach to understanding a research assignment is a powerful tool for use by savvy associates to ensure that they fully understand a new research assignment. It prompts you to ask valuable questions at the beginning of the project, as opposed to asking the important questions after significant billable hours have been spent or when the deadline is looming. Going back to the above hypothetical, an associate using the J.U.S.T. A.S.K. approach would have asked a series of probing questions that would have helped him or her understand the project despite the supervisor's initially vague or incomplete instructions. (One other note: *As with all other assignments, always ask the supervisor for the client/matter number for a particular research assignment to ensure your time, photocopying and any Westlaw charges are properly billed.*)

By the way, did you ask the partner for the name and fax number of her hotel where the memorandum is to be sent by 7 a.m.? J.U.S.T. A.S.K. is a great tool, but it can't remind you to ask about everything! You are becoming a *From Finals to the Firm* veteran by following our tips to guide your career, but never forget common sense!

Before You Start Your Research ... *"J.U.S.T. A.S.K."**

Jurisdiction

> Find out if you need to examine federal or state, court or administrative decisions, regulatory or legislative sources or some combination.

Useful tips

> The assigning attorney may know of experts in the field, recent publications, or internal documents that could help you. Try to get names of people, and copies or cites of documents.

Scope

> How much information is the attorney really looking for? Should your research be exhaustive or just an overview?

Terms of art

> Ask the assigning attorney for standard terms of art and their definitions. Knowing the right terminology can save time, effort and money.

Acronyms

> Clarify the spelling and meaning of acronyms. Attorneys in specialized fields tend to throw these around without realizing they may be meaningless to those new to the field.

Sources

> As an expert, the assigning attorney should know the "bibles" of research in the field. Ask for titles of key journals, loose-leafs, treatises, and databases.

* Adopted from "JUST ASK" © 1993 Ellen Callinan, Georgetown University Law Center.

Key cost constraints

Is the client a stickler on certain charges, such as Westlaw? How many hours should you be billing on this project? Can you use faxes, document delivery services and messengers? Find out before you start spending.

SIDEBAR TO NO. 5

DeMaurice F. Smith, Esq.
B.A. Cedarville College; J.D. with honors, University of Virginia
Partner, Patton Boggs LLP, Washington, D.C.

Moral of the Sidebar: Context is King

I would offer only one modification to the advice given in this chapter about when to best understand a research assignment. In addition to being the *best* time to understand the project, the pace of a law firm and the multitasking nature of most partner work mean that the beginning of an assignment may be the *only* time you get to truly understand it.

What many associates do not realize is that once a research matter is assigned, many partners check that issue off of their ever expanding "to do" list and move on to the next crisis. Accordingly, the review of the work (which may not take place for days after the completion) is rarely done in the context of what was told to the associate at the time or even the information that the partner believed was being conveyed at the time. In addition to unpacking all of the critical elements or data points in order to understand and respond to the assignment, it is incumbent on the associate to understand the context in which this matter is being requested. For example, is it for a portion of the due diligence review, a term or issue for a contract, a question by the client, a jurisdictional or venue issue for a complaint, a choice of law inquiry or for specific jury instructions or briefing to the court. The context is the critical issue because it not only serves as a foil to elicit details necessary to "get the right answer," it is an important factor in understanding the expectation of the assigner and the level of detail or final product that you are being asked to render.

After you understand the context there are several critical mistakes to avoid.

First, this is no longer a law school environment. The issue of jurisdiction is not only an important touchstone, but it is also one of the critical issues for defining the analytical framework. Although one can write the comprehensive law review article on a variety of issues, the "value added" for costly research is the ability to have the results tailored to the client's precise circumstance.

Accordingly, the real measure of the work is not the volume of the reply, but the precision and accuracy of the analysis.

Today, we do not suffer from a lack of potential resources for answers to questions. A mere Google search of a potential topic is likely to turn up thousands of potential reference points. The tailoring process is what you can seek to get from the partners when you raise specific articles or resources of which they may be aware. But it is equally important to ensure that this is not your only data point—you should seek additional or even contrary cites or discussions of the issue. If I had to identify one factor that distinguishes law school from the "real world" it's that there is virtually never a time in the real world when you are not an advocate in your analysis. Clients are looking for a competitive advantage everywhere, regardless of whether it is a business trans-action, litigation, Government investigation or even a lobbying or public policy question. The associate who distinguishes herself is the one who recognizes that the answer may be apparent, but the advocacy and argument is where she can add significant value.

While we are talking about distinctions between law school and the real world, let's take notice of another significant real world factor: *cost.* Associates who ignore the cost of their work in relation to the legal budget for that task do so at their own peril. This is another critical mistake to avoid. The downside of being a senior partner (at least from my perspective) is the non-legal and administrative work that consumes the practice. Clients, whether individuals or corpora-tions, perceive legal costs as primarily overhead and typically an expense item which rarely makes them money. As a partner, you continually face issues relating to the budget for work overall, the itemized expenditures per attorney and the budgetary expectations of your clients. Associates should be aware of these tensions as well, even if they do not review or send bills to clients. At the inception of any research assignment, follow the contextual analysis with a discussion of the cost constraints and client expectations. Most of our clients are businesses who continuously engage in the cost/ben-efit analysis of the work they require or ask to be done. If those expectations are inconsistent with the deliverable (either in content or cost) you will have client discontent *even if the answers were correct.*

Finally, every good associate learns that the deliverable is only as good as its reliability. Whether you are asked to provide an answer, take a position or evaluate an argument, there is a careful balance between having confidence in your position and being able to defend it, and stubbornly resisting critical analysis. I am continu-ously amazed by the reaction I get at times from associates when I challenge their findings or conclusions. I certainly understand the hard work they put in or the dedication and belief they have in the conclusions. Nonetheless, the proving ground for the analysis (for which we expect to be handsomely paid) is critical thinking and an analysis colored by experience as well as reason. This is exactly what the client expects.

Our job as service providers is to manage expectations by evaluating all of the factors that are important to the people for which we work. By asking questions "up front", by employing the proper analysis and understanding—both the research project and context in which it is asked and will be delivered—young associates will find themselves well on the path to partnership.

NO. 6: BE A COMPLETE PLAYER

Have you ever gone to the gym and seen a mammoth guy walk by with his neck bulging out of his T-shirt, arms like carved steel and a chest like a bear? Then, as your eyes scan down, you notice that he has skinny legs like a Paris runway model? Or, as you spend time on the treadmill, you see muscle-bound people walk by who never do any cardiovascular work? You know, the same people who can lift the entire rack of weights, but can't run a city block without gasping for air? Well the above-described persons are not complete players in their game—fitness. You must not emulate them while being an associate at a firm. Rather, you want to be like Mike!

Michael Jordan is widely considered the best basketball player of all time not only because he was dominant on offense (*i.e.*, as a scorer), but he was a feared defensive player! He became that complete player through countless hours of practicing. Similarly, during your time at the firm, you must master all facets of firm life in order to be successful. You must be a complete player in the firm game. Building your talent, fostering a good image and getting proper exposure (*i.e.*, T.I.E.ing) will get you partially there, but not all the way. In order to be a complete player in the law firm game you must: (1) socialize (both at the bar and at the Bar); (2) avoid burning bridges; and (3) practice, practice, practice!

Socialize

Do not make the common mistake of underestimating the value of socializing. It is an important part of being a complete player at the firm. You can't just "do good work," go home and think that your rise to partnership will be guaranteed. You must spend time at the "bar" when you're at the firm. More specifically, you need to spend time at Bar Association activities and spend time hanging out with fellow associates and partners at the bar (*i.e.*, the kind that serves drinks).

The Bar

A fair amount of business gets done at social functions. Social time at the firm is a key time to get to know your colleagues in a setting that isn't filled with work-related pressure. It is also a good time to learn about new project opportunities, firm-related trends and firm-specific "tricks of the trade." We realize that you may not think, at least initially, that your law firm colleagues are the coolest people in the world. You've noticed that many of them don't listen to the same music that you do, don't come from the same background as you or even have the same interests.

Well, get over it! You need to make, at a minimum, casual friendships at the firm in order to be plugged in to what's going on. If that includes going to the bar and ordering a soft drink while everyone is downing liquor, putting your suit in the cleaners the next day to get rid of the cigarette and cigar smoke and smiling at a couple of lame jokes, so be it! (You may even end up telling a few lame jokes yourself and finding out that you're not the coolest one of the bunch after all.) Don't take our advice to socialize too literally though. Our advice to socialize applies to other social activities such as leaving the office to grab a cup of coffee with a colleague.

You must use social functions to get to know your colleagues better, let them see you as someone they can trust and like on a basic level and, quite frankly, to at least hear the latest buzz about the firm. Being a complete player means that you must attend at least a few of the different types of firm functions. These include the summer associate gatherings, that dreaded party at the senior partner's house (should you be lucky enough to be invited) and, of course, the firm's big holiday party. This is not to say you need to attend *every* function *all* the time. You should, however, be occasionally seen on the scene so that you're not perceived as not being "one of us" or "part of the team."

As always, we offer some precautionary notes. First, let us remind you that everyone is still watching you at these social gatherings. Second, before going to any event, get a sense of the dress code. You don't want to be the guy in a golf shirt, shorts and sneakers at the partner's summer picnic when everyone else is wearing a sport coat, slacks and shoes. You don't want to be the woman at the firm dinner wearing the sexy red dress when every other woman is wearing more conservative business attire. Lastly, don't feel free to get drunk enough to do your best impression of Britney Spears' latest music video dance routine. Socializing can easily be taken too far! That is, don't drink to the point where you might do or say something you will later regret.

The Bar Association

Your city or metropolitan area most likely has several local bar associations and local chapters of national bar associations. All of these organizations may have events in or near the city where you work. There will also be more narrowly-tailored bar associations (or committees within larger bar associations) that cater specifically to your field of interest or focus on issues related to certain groups. These associations are a great resource to network with like-minded legal professionals and to gain valuable insights on the progression of their careers.

Participating in bar associations is also a valuable tool for making contacts with people who might work at a firm that ultimately fits you better than your current firm. In 2006, the national attrition rate at U.S. law firms was 19% and nearly 80% of all associates leave their firm by the end of five years.[4] (Remember, always have an exit strategy—be your own angel!) Thus, the person sitting next to you at the next bar seminar might be your next boss or even outside mentor, future client or source of your next referral (maybe even your future spouse)! These associations and their committees may also allow you to get exposure to other firms and practice areas that you have not been able to get exposed to at your current firm.

Burning Bridges

Overall, you must master the entire (law firm) game in order to be a successful associate. Being a complete player who plays the whole game includes not burning bridges with people whom you do not work well, don't respect or don't like. For example, if you don't do well on a project, go back to the supervisor and sincerely ask for another one, promise to do better, and then actually do better. It is almost never a good idea to badmouth a supervisor or colleague to others. What if that person is a good friend of the person you're badmouthing and you don't even know it? What if that person becomes a future client or future boss of yours? Then what will you do?

Practice Makes ...

Finally, in order to be a complete player, you must practice because, just like in any other context, practice makes perfect.

As we mentioned above, Michael Jordan, despite being endowed with tremendous talent, became the best basketball player ever by practicing relentlessly, continuing to minimize his weaknesses and adding new components to his game over the course of his playing career. To be a successful young associate, you too must practice! Now, you may ask, "How in the world do I *practice* at the firm?" Well, practicing does not mean sitting in your office writing fictional briefs for current Supreme Court cases. "Practicing," in the law firm context, means doing things that will allow you to build your talent without necessarily taking the risks that are

---

4. Elizabeth Goldberg, *Moving On Inevitable for Many Midlevels*, National   Law Journal Online (Aug. 17, 2006) (*quoting* statistics gathered by NALP).

associated with working for paying clients. Practicing means reading your local bar magazine or journal, reading the daily, weekly or monthly digest that is focused on the practice areas in which you're interested. For example, Calvin—a real estate associate—read *The Practical Real Estate Lawyer*, a bimonthly quick-read pamphlet, to keep him briefed on trends in real estate. (You should recall that in Chapter 3 we advised you to find out which journals, magazines, advance sheets, *etc.* the attorneys in your practice area(s) often read.)

Practicing also means searching the firm's computer document management system for documents that a partner or senior associate you are working for has previously drafted. Reviewing these examples before drafting a new agreement, pleading or memorandum will allow you to understand the substance and style with which that supervisor is comfortable. It's the equivalent of an aspiring basketball professional watching videotapes of a current star in order to incorporate some of their moves! Somebody right now is watching tapes of LeBron James, who watched tapes of Kobe Bryant, who watched tapes of Michael Jordan! Reviewing a supervisor's or star associate's previous work product is an easy way to obtain a road map for successfully drafting good work for your supervisor.

Practicing can also mean taking on and being successful at *pro bono* work. *Pro bono* work can be an excellent way for a young associate to get exposure to complex legal challenges prior to the point where partners may allow you to do the same for paying clients. *We don't use the term "practice" with respect to pro bono work to imply that you should be any less diligent while representing your pro bono clients than your paying clients.* We simply mean that representing *pro bono* clients may give you additional opportunities to build your talent without the risk of failing in front of a paying client (or opportunities to try new practice areas). You may be able to fully handle a case from the initial pleadings to hearings to settlement *years* before the firm would afford you a similar opportunity for a paying client. That *pro bono* case could allow you to build the talent necessary to be able to convince the partner that you can do that deposition for Client, Inc. because you've done similar depositions for *pro bono* clients.

In sum, go have a drink (or a cup of coffee) with your co-workers, attend a bar association function, say "hello" to the partner whose brief you had to re-write twice and pick up a *pro bono* client. Remember, only complete players get voted M.V.P.!

NO. 7: THINK OUTSIDE
THE BOX

So you are now in law firm heaven. You've found an angel. You're being your own angel. As a matter of fact, you find that partners are now coming to you for advice! (Okay, well maybe not). All in all, after reading the first six chapters, you are well on your way to becoming a successful law firm associate. In the next three chapters we continue beefing up your arsenal of tricks of the trade with some advanced insider secrets. The first of these insider secrets that we address you've heard many times before: "Think outside the box." Generally, "thinking outside of the box" means solving a problem using a unique approach, angle or method of analysis. Below, we will apply this problem-solving methodology in a way that helps you, while you're being your own angel, stand out among your peers at the firm.

Adjectives Versus Nouns

"*Patent* attorney." "*Tax* attorney." "*Real estate* attorney." "*Corporate* attorney." "*Employment* attorney." Within the law firm, there are going to be people who describe themselves using these titles. In time, as you become more senior and settle into a specialty at the firm, you too will start using these titles to describe yourself. Do not, however, be fooled by such nomenclature. Raymond may at times call himself a "*patent* attorney." He realizes, however, that "patent" is simply the adjective, and "attorney" is the noun. First and foremost he is an "attorney." Thus, when he analyzes a client's problem, he doesn't just think "patent," "patent," and "patent." Similarly, Calvin calls himself a "*real estate* attorney." He realizes, however, that "real estate" is simply the adjective, and "attorney" is the noun. Thus, when he analyzes a client's problem, he doesn't just think "real estate," "real estate," and "real estate." The "box" you need to think outside of is your area of specialty.

Putting the above in other words, the lesson to be learned is that you should never practice your legal specialty in a vacuum.

There's a real world out there. So, no matter what kind of attorney you are, you have to think of yourself as an *attorney* first. Clients come to you to solve real-life problems and those problems don't always confine themselves—like law school exams—to one specific area of the law.

Regardless of whether your firm advertises itself as a "boutique," you are not selling clothes! Clients pay you for a unique service. That unique service is the application of your professional judgment to their problems. So every time you bill a tenth of an hour to a client, don't forget what your clients are really paying for—your professional judgment. (We discuss client billing in a bit more detail in Chapter 10.) That judgment must be an informed one. So, as you go through your career attempting to learn as many aspects of your chosen legal practice area as possible, you also have to seek out knowledge about other areas of law that often intersect with your chosen practice area. This allows you to give your clients comprehensive legal advice. You'll be amazed at how often clients will depend on you as simply their *attorney* (*i.e.*, the noun) to solve their problems and care less that you call yourself a *"labor* attorney" (*i.e.*, they'll care little about the adjective).

Spotting the Issues

How do you apply the above lesson? Well, recall law school final exams for just one moment, and you'll remember that the ability to "issue spot" was half the battle towards getting an "A" grade. The same is true in practicing law. But, unlike those law school final exams, the next project may not be about just one topic (*e.g.*, torts, contracts or criminal law). For example, if you're working on a patent licensing transaction, there may be tax, corporate or even antitrust implications. If you're working on a corporate merger or acquisition, there may be employment, environmental or intellectual property law issues that arise. If you're working on a real estate deal, tax or corporate issues may arise. You get the picture!

Now, we are not advocating that you attempt to become an expert in every area of the law. Should you be able to do that, then great! But, for the other 99.8% of you, we mean to say that you must: "Know enough to know when you don't know enough!" In other words, *you must develop enough of an understanding about the other areas of the law that frequently intersect the specialty in which you practice, in order to recognize when those other areas become implicated and then seek assistance.* (The same can be said for your chosen practice area—be careful to recognize when you need help from someone more senior.)

When you spot an issue from another area of the law and realize that you don't know enough about that area to address it yourself, and if you practice at a firm with multiple practice groups, you can call the other attorneys at the firm from those other practice groups. Then, you can say: "Hey, I have a situation where X, and I was wondering whether this raises Y and Z implications from your area of the law?" The other attorney may assure you that there's no issue or may suggest an easy solution. The other attorney may suggest that additional research needs to be done to properly analyze and address the issue. By having this discussion, you are providing the client with value-added services and increasing your exposure to other areas of the firm. Further, not only have you just addressed the client's total needs as their "attorney" (*i.e.,* a noun), you have just engaged in what firms like to call "cross selling" (*i.e.,* selling a client legal services across practice group boundaries, thereby increasing revenue for the firm).

As usual, we offer some words of caution. It is not our intention for you to raise issues that are not there, thereby needlessly inflating clients' bills! In your early years of practice, you should ask your supervisor or a more senior associate in your practice area whether the "out of the box" issue that you spotted is one that requires further analysis. This will allow you to: (a) avoid talking to a specialist within the firm before there is really a need to further analyze the issue; and (b) get the "go-ahead" from your supervisor before incurring additional billable hours on the project.

Oftentimes, associates flag an issue but are directed to spend no further time on it by the supervisor because the client has cost constraints (more on this in Chapter 10) or because the issue is not that important (*i.e.,* there is not likely to be any serious negative ramifications for the client even if the issue is not addressed). As a new associate you want to do your best to ensure that your supervisor is never surprised by the amount of hours billed to a client matter, and you don't want billable time from other attorneys within the firm showing up on internal timesheets unless that additional time has been pre-approved by the supervisor. You can get the go-ahead from your supervisor with a quick phone call or e-mail. Supervisors and clients will appreciate the fact that you asked before you plunged forward. The bottom line, however, is that you always have to be "thinking outside the box" so that you can spot intersecting issues outside of your practice area when they are present. That is, you have to understand that you don't practice your area of the law in a vacuum and that some areas of the law frequently implicate other areas of the law. *Know enough to know when you don't know enough!*

NO. 8: C.Y.A.

If you have never heard or seen the acronym "C.Y.A.," it stands for "cover your @$$!" (Do we really need to spell out the last word for you?) As an attorney you will often be instructed to avoid leaving a paper trail. Examples include the shredding of preliminary drafts or prior versions of documents, properly (and legally) disposing of papers that may contain client confidences and using discretion when distributing documents or correspondence via e-mail. There are times, however, when you do want to leave a paper trail. There are times when you *need* to leave a paper trail in order to C.Y.A. Why? The following story will shed some light.

The Case of the Missing Paper Trail

Let's say tomorrow is the statute of limitations for filing a certain action and the client gives you a call at 5:00 p.m. and says: "You know, we've thought about it and the board of directors doesn't want to file that case anymore." Then you reply, "Okay, fine." A couple of weeks (or even a couple of months) later, a partner says to you: "Wait a minute, we never filed that action. Why not?" To which you confidently reply, "The client called me and told me not to." The partner gets on the telephone with the client, and the client says: "We never said that! Who did your associate speak to and when?" Naturally, the partner passes this question on to you, and naturally, you don't have a clue as to the answer. Those countless, consecutive twelve-hour days have left your brain fried and your memory useless. Unfortunately, "I spoke to somebody, uh, I think it was a guy, a couple of weeks ago," is not a sufficient answer to the partner's question. You look bad, the partner looks bad, the firm looks bad and the client isn't happy. You may have also bought the firm a malpractice lawsuit!

Does the above scenario sound like a nightmare? Is being a clueless and unorganized associate the image you want to convey? What did you do wrong? After all, you just followed directions. Well, you didn't C.Y.A.! You never wrote a memorandum to the file indicating that John Doe, CFO of Client, Inc., told you not to file that lawsuit on October 15 during a conversation that lasted from

5:00 p.m. to 5:05 p.m. Get the picture? In addition, since you know that you have zero authority to execute a client's decision, you probably should call or e-mail your supervisor immediately so that they are aware of the client's latest instructions. It's possible that your supervisor will call the client to discuss the decision. Either way, you're covered.

Put simply, the moral of the above story is if you don't leave a paper trail (*e.g.*, a memorandum to the file that states on a certain date, you spoke to a certain person and they told you to take or not to take a certain action), you cannot provide the client and the partner with the pertinent information and, just as importantly, you cannot C.Y.A.! You are your own angel. So, guess who should be covering your ... uh ... derriere? You! That is, you must always document important instructions received, whether by placing a memorandum in the file to document a telephone call or printing an e-mail containing instructions from the client, and placing it in the file. (Many firms have pre-printed telephone memorandum pads or word processor-specific templates on the local computer network for this precise reason.)

C.Y.A. Scenarios

While the above story is one example of a C.Y.A. scenario, it is not exhaustive. Whenever a client says "don't file that complaint," "let that statute of limitations run," "don't depose that witness," "leave out that important clause in the contract," "don't spend the money for that," *etc.*, you want to document those instructions in the file to C.Y.A.

Aside from the above examples, the concept of C.Y.A. also comes into play in other ways. You sometimes need to C.Y.A. to have a record of who is holding up progress on a particular project (*i.e.*, which party has not completed their responsibility within the project). For example, you may be negotiating a deal or be involved in a matter where you interact with opposing counsel. Consider what would happen if you send a contract to opposing counsel and weeks go by without a response? What would happen if you spoke to opposing counsel and they promised to forward a document that never comes? What would happen if you send an e-mail to a partner with an answer to a question they posed and you receive no response? In each of the previous circumstances, the partner (or even the client) may think any resulting delays are your fault. How do you counter that negative impression and rebuild your image? The answer is C.Y.A.! Every time you've done your part and placed the ball in someone else's court, document it by creating a telephone memorandum or placing a copy of the e-mail or cover letter (and any attachments) in the file. Even if you are working on a small part of a larger matter and you don't have access to the actual file, create a "dummy file" for that matter, place copies of all the documents you touched in it and keep it in your office. In the end, you will be able to pull out copies of the e-mails, letters, telephone memoranda, *etc.* that you need to show (politely) that you're no slacker! We should reiterate, however, that you shouldn't simply create a C.Y.A. file, put it away and let the chips fall where they may. A quick phone call or e-mail to alert your supervisor may also be warranted in many situations.

In the end, you may not only be saving your butt from a partner's wrath, but you may be saving the firm from malpractice liability as well (*i.e.*, clients may sometimes forget what they have instructed you to do). In time, as you become a more senior associate and more comfortable and versed in the practice of law, you will become savvy in recognizing when to C.Y.A., how to C.Y.A., and with whom you need to be most prepared to C.Y.A.

Y.C.Y.A.?

Why else should you C.Y.A.? First, to be frank, you should C.Y.A. because when the feces hits the fan, you don't want any blame to be apportioned to you because you don't have the evidence to support your side of the story. As a new associate you do not have the authority to make (most, if any) important decisions regarding strategy. Therefore, you should have a documented history of who made the decisions.

Second, you always want to build your image as the most organized person on the team. Guess who gets the "Most Organized Award" when you are the only one who has a copy of the e-mail that shows the client chose, over the firm's objection, to accept a certain money-losing provision in a contract and now they are unhappy? Lastly, you should C.Y.A. because it is a great backup for your limited ability to remember *anything* about a deal that closed, or a brief that was filed, three years ago (or even three months ago). Having the answer on paper will save you from your own limited capabilities to remember every detail about every matter you've ever worked on!

There Is a Method to the Madness

Caution: Always pay particular attention to what you place in client matter files! You only need to document the basic facts (*i.e.*, the instructions) of a communication to C.Y.A. A detailed analysis (*i.e.*, the legal reasoning or motivation) of the communication is not necessary, and oftentimes not prudent. You never know what may end up being produced during discovery in a later litigation. For example, compare:

Good C.Y.A. Memorandum Entry:

October 15, 5:00–5:10 p.m., Jane Doe, CFO of Client, Inc., called to instruct us to close matter.

Versus:

Bad C.Y.A. Memorandum Entry:

October 15, 5:00–5:10 p.m., Jane Doe, CFO of Client, Inc., called to instruct us to close matter because our legal position is not the best given the facts we have and Other Side, Inc. would surely win if we proceeded.

You should now get the point!

The "Good Work" File

There is one more kind of paper trail that we need to tell you about. At first blush, what we are about to tell you may seem a bit paranoid. Our response, using the words of a senior partner that Raymond worked for early in his career, is that: "Only the paranoid survive!" This kind of C.Y.A. is what we call keeping a "good work" file.

A good work file is something that, if your time at the firm goes smoothly, you may never need to use. However, being paranoid, it's always good to know it's there. Soon after your arrival at the firm, we recommend placing an empty file in your bottom-desk drawer and labeling it "Good Work File." Every time you get an e-mail or letter from a client saying, "great job," print it out or photocopy it and put it in your good work file. Every time a partner sends you an e-mail saying, "you know, thanks a lot for that brief, it was awesome," print it out and put it in your good work file. As time goes on, your good work file should hopefully be more than the one millimeter in thickness that it was when you first started at the firm.

Don't get us wrong. We are not advocating sending out e-mails or letters to clients and partners to solicit good work file contents. We are only advocating that you file unsolicited praise and recognition of your hard work and talent. This also includes review forms that senior associates and partners may have to fill out for you as part of your firm's formal review process. (If your firm's process allows you to obtain copies of these forms, the ones with positive comments should be photocopied and placed in your good work file.)

It's Not for "Ego Tripping" with Friends

What is the purpose of this good work file? Well, the answer is simple. Most firms have an annual or semi-annual associate review process. During that process, as part of being your own angel, you have to be your own best advocate. You have to go in there and justify why you should receive the top available bonus, why you should get a raise (or the top available raise), why you should get the nice office, *etc.* When you go in to the review meeting, go armed with your good work file. If your review goes well, the existence of your good work file need not be revealed. If there are inaccuracies, however, this is where your good work file comes in handy. At this point you need to use your good work file wisely (and diplomatically) to correct those inaccuracies.

Lastly, if your practice group, department or firm as a whole happens to be going through tough times and not all the associates are being kept busy with assignments, or should you find that work is not finding its way to your in-box, you need to document your efforts to seek out work. The e-mails and/or memos documenting conversations seeking projects to work on should also be placed in your good work file. This will allow you, if the need arises later in the year, to justify why you fell short of the firm's minimum billable hours requirement.

One last paranoid note. Should you ever find yourself unjustifiably fired, forget all the beautifully framed diplomas on the wall or sentimental trinkets on your bookshelves! The only thing you're ever going to need to take with you as you're being escorted out by security (don't worry, this is extremely rare) is your good work file! (One of our seminar attendees suggested keeping the good work file "off premises" for this very reason. Boy, paranoia is really contagious!)

NO. 9: GO GET THE BELT

We just shared with you that practicing law is a business. Well, while growing up, our parents considered running the household a business as well! As such, if threats of moral doom and damnation didn't bring about behavior conducive to making the household run smoothly, our parents often resorted to a more corporeal method to bring about corrective action—a good old-fashioned spanking! As a matter of fact, Calvin's mom would add the psychological to the physical by ordering Calvin to obtain the instrument of his own punishment. That is, he would be ordered to: "Go get the belt!"

In the law firm context, we cannot advocate that you pull out the old leather strap the next time your supervisor sends you on a three-week assignment looking through an old warehouse for documents to be produced in a litigation. What we do advocate, however, is that you seek out constructive criticism from your supervisors and that you make sure that the constructive criticism goes both ways. That is what we mean by: "Go get the belt!"

Seeking Constructive Criticism

Unfortunately, your supervisor probably did not take a course entitled "Supervisor 101" in law school, nor did they register for the "How to Give Constructive Feedback to New Associates" continuing legal education (CLE) class. In fact, it is not uncommon for younger associates to feel that the partners at their firm do not know how to supervise and develop associates, or to feel that the partners are not nearly as interested in their professional development as they claimed to be (especially when considering the usual promises made during the recruiting process).[5] Thus, it is your job as a new associate to obtain constructive feedback that will help you become successful in your law firm career.

Face it, your supervisor is going to be very busy. He's balancing billing his 2000+ hours and supervising you—ye of little faith

---

5. Joel A. Rose, *What Partners Can Learn from Associates About Retaining* *Top Quality Associates*, 25 No. 8 Of Counsel 5 (Aug. 2006).

and even less knowledge. So when you finish that research memorandum or new document that you spent fifty billable hours working on, he may not think to give you feedback on your performance. He may not tell you that you did a great job finding the relevant cases, but that you did not effectively back up your ultimate conclusion. If it was a corporate transactional document, maybe he didn't tell you that some of the terms you used were undefined and that it was apparent that you blindly "cut and pasted" some provisions from another document that were inapplicable to the current deal. Oftentimes, your supervisor may simply make the changes they feel are necessary and send the document out to the client without mentioning to you that there were areas to improve. Worse, the supervisor may send the document out without discussing it with you and then tell his fellow partners or senior associates that you produced a shoddy work product.

What can you do? How will you know? Well, you must go get the belt! It is important to seek out constructive criticism during the course of, and immediately after, a project. This will, at a minimum, help you avoid similar mistakes in the future or, at a maximum, allow you to correct mistakes before you become the topic of negative bar room conversation. For example, it is possible that the supervisor would have returned the document for you to correct if you had asked him for feedback when you turned it in and made it clear that you were willing to spend whatever amount of time necessary to correct the document. In the all too often frantic pace of law firm life, there isn't always time for you to receive feedback and fix mistakes during the project, but at least you have communicated to the supervisor that you want constructive feedback so that you can do a better job next time. Receiving positive and negative feedback not only will help you build your talent, but it will also assist you in avoiding nicks in your meticulously polished image so that you can get crucial future exposure. (*Remember that the only reward for good work is more work!*)

In seeking constructive criticism, you need to ascertain not only what you did wrong, but also what you did right! Understanding your strengths on a project is important so that you can replicate that success in future projects. Moreover, recognizing the things you do best may help you select the area of practice you may want to eventually settle into at the firm. For example, if your supervisor says that you did an excellent job drafting the financing terms for a real estate sale, but did poorly drafting the real estate-specific terms, maybe you should consider trying more banking or lender-related work that play to your strengths. You should compare any feedback you receive to your own personal interests. This comparison will guide you towards work that is not only interesting to you, but in which you can be most successful.

You want your supervisor to know that you are asking for feedback because you want to make sure you did a good job, want to get their input on your performance and that you want to do more work for them in the future! Okay, maybe he was the supervisor from hell and you don't EVER want to work for him again. You still want and need that supervisor's feedback and, as we discussed in Chapter 6, *you never want to burn bridges.* You may never work for that supervisor again; but you don't want him badmouthing you to the supervisors you actually do want to work for in the future!

The Right Questions, at the Right Time, in the Right Way

You need to be savvy about how and when you approach supervisors for constructive criticism. *The best feedback is received during the project so that you can make corrections before you have to submit your final work product.* However, if the deal is about to close this week or the brief is due tomorrow; maybe you should wait a day or two before asking probing questions. You should ask succinct, yet specific questions about your performance and try to get specific answers in return. Asking, "How'd I do?" or "How was it?" may only elicit a quick "Fine." But asking your supervisor: "Did my memorandum analyze the relevant cases in a way that was helpful and correct?" Or, asking: "Did my draft properly capture all of the business terms and legal issues?" may elicit a more specific and measured response. You want to ask these types of questions in a way that shows that you care about your work product, you care about the supervisor's opinion and that you want to become a better attorney. A more open-ended question which might elicit a specific response could be: "What were the best things about my performance on your assignment and what are the things you think I can improve on in the future?" Hopefully, that question will let your supervisor know that you want to make sure you did a good job, want to get their input on your performance and that you want to do more work for them in the future!

If you know that you did poorly on a particular assignment, the time to seek out the supervisor is right away. Actually, it is more important for you to talk to your supervisor after doing a bad job than after doing a good job! Asking for specific feedback will show that you care about the fact you didn't do your best work, and that you take responsibility for your mistakes and want to improve. Ask them how you can rectify the situation if the mistake or assignment is not final or complete. Owning up to your mistakes and asking for a second chance is the sign of a mature associate who is willing to work hard to become a successful attorney. Most supervisors will appreciate your sincerity.

To be frank, there are certain supervisors who will, regardless of how appropriately you ask for feedback, not be amenable, approachable or accessible. That's not necessarily a personal knock on these supervisors. Remember, they are usually not trained on how to give proper feedback and may be uncomfortable or uncertain how to constructively give you positive and negative feedback, or just plainly overworked. It is your job as your own CEO, however, to coax feedback out of them without turning it into a big thing. One trick of the trade is to do some investigating in order to obtain your feedback. For example, if the supervisor did not return the document for you to correct and you know it was filed with the court or sent out to the client, find the final version. If your firm uses a document management system, it is easy (if you're being your own CTO) to compare the draft you submitted to your supervisor with the final version on the system.

If your firm does not use a document management system, just remember Chapter 4—the staff is it! That is, ask the supervisor's secretary for the supervisor's verbal reaction to your submitted draft. An even better idea is to ask the supervisor's secretary for a copy of the "markup." That is, most supervisors will make hand-written edits on your typewritten draft of a document and hand it to their secretary to input the desired changes—these are called "markups." Although reviewing your supervisor's markup is not as good as receiving first-hand feedback, it will give you a sense of what the supervisor liked and disliked about your work product. Moreover, you should sometimes keep copies of markups given to you by your supervisor for editing. For example, if you know you are going to have to draft or analyze a similar document in the future, you can use the supervisor's markup as a rough guide to possible arguments or points you need to make when you receive a draft of a similar document from opposing counsel. Many of the supervisor's changes in your markup may be relevant to your analysis of the new document. However, don't blindly make the same comments as your supervisor. Instead, review the old markup and ascertain whether any of the old comments are relevant considering the business terms and legal issues present in the new assignment.

Class-Appropriate Progress is Key

One key thing to focus on when asking for feedback from supervisors is *whether your performance—which will most often be a combination of good and not so good—was appropriate for your level as an associate*. Supervisors will often forget to specify whether their feedback is positive or negative and whether it shows you are on pace with where you should be at your level (*i.e.*, associate class year). So the fact that the supervisor said you only made "one or two major errors on the document" does not tell you whether an associate of your class year usually makes *no* errors on that type of document and therefore you actually didn't do so well on the project. Conversely, if the supervisor says you only made one or two errors on a document but, when asked, notes that so few errors is the type of work product that a more senior associate might produce, you know that you are doing a good job and are at pace with, or ahead of, your class year in the progression of your lawyering skills. In sum, always put feedback in perspective and don't let negative feedback get you down.

Constructive Criticism is a Two–Way Street

In an appropriate and tactful way, you need to *supervise your supervisor*. In other words, you need to let them know what are the things you need them to do in order for you to do your best job on the project. Supervising your supervisor, at first, may sound silly. After all, the partners and senior associates are the supervisors for a reason, no? Well, yes they have more *legal* experience. However, "[t]oo often, firms allow partners and other senior lawyers the opportunity to manage associates with little guidance about how to effectively communicate with associates, how to provide feedback in a constructive way, how to motivate associates and inspire interest in their work."[6] So, faced with this law firm reality, how do you go about supervising your supervisor?

As we stated earlier, the best feedback is given and received during the project, or right after. You also, where appropriate, want to tactfully let them know the things they could have done differently which would have resulted in a better work product from you. Now remember, at the end of the day, you are the associate (*i.e.*, an employee terminable at will) and they are the boss. So don't get pushy, and don't start wagging your finger at the supervisor telling them, "if you put as much time in the office as you do on the golf course, maybe you would have been around to help out!" Instead, you might ask the supervisor what is the best method for you to contact them—whether they'd prefer that you come to their office to ask questions, send them an e-mail or even if it is appropriate to contact them on their mobile phone if a mission-critical issue arises? Turn questions around so that you are not being confrontational—regardless of whether the supervisor is on the golf course while you're stressing out and pounding away back at the office.

Belt in Hand

Overall, going to get the belt (*i.e.*, seeking out and giving constructive criticism and feedback) is another tool to increase and improve communication between you and your supervisor. It is also

---

6. Kristin K. Stark and Blane Prescott, *Why Associates Leave*, Legal Times (May 7, 2007).

a method of focusing on your T.I.E. (*i.e.*, building your *talent*, fostering the right *image* and gaining crucial *exposure*). When seeking out and giving feedback, be specific. Give the type of feedback and constructive criticism you would like to receive in return. Cite examples if you have to jog their memory. Tell them what you think a better process might have been. Ask them what they think about your ideas. You want to do more listening than talking. You want to be sincere about your willingness to accept your mistakes. You want to be sincere about your desire to understand your strengths and weaknesses, and sincere about wanting to do better the next time. In the end, maybe the belt won't hurt that much after all.

NO. 10: LEARN THE BUSINESS OF PRACTICING

In Chapter 4, we mentioned that you probably have never taken a personnel management class. Well, we're going to go out on a limb and guess that you've also never taken a law firm economics class. We hate to break the bad news to you, but practicing law is a business! And like all other businesses, the goal is to make money! Think about it: Can the firm afford to pay you the first-year associate salary that caught your attention during the recruitment process if it wasn't a profitable concern!? So let's look at some basic law firm economics.

Your Salary

We start "Law Firm Economics 101" with a subject you care a lot about—your salary. How can many of these firms pay such handsome first-year associate salaries to lawyers who have no legal experience and, basically, know next to nothing!? Well, the answer involves understanding how the "minimum billable hour" and the "billing rate" relate to your salary. In explaining how to be your own angel, we told you: "Never leave money on the table!" That is, we advised that you must always attempt to meet the firm's minimum billable hours requirement. Let's explore once more—this time from the firm's partnership perspective—why meeting the minimum billable hour requirement is important. We'll use the following example to guide us, and while doing so, we will try not to terribly aggravate your phobia of mathematics.

The minute you step through the door at the firm, you are assigned a billing rate. Let's say it is $175 per hour. That is, if you spend ten hours doing legal research and drafting a memorandum for a partner, the client has just incurred a bill for $1,750. (This assumes, of course, that you were efficient and the entire ten hours are actually billed out to the client by the partner.)

To add to our example, let's say your starting salary is $100,000 per year and the firm has an 1800–hour minimum billable hours requirement. The question becomes how does the firm set that minimum billable hour requirement? Well a general (and admittedly rough) rule of thumb that many firms follow is that for each dollar an associate generates: one-third goes towards the associate's salary, one-third goes to overhead (*e.g.*, space, staff salaries, benefits, *etc.*) and one-third goes to the partnership (*i.e.*, profits). So, if you bill 1800 hours a year at $175 per hour, you have just generated $315,000 for the firm. Of that $315,000, roughly one-third goes towards your salary of $100,000 per year. (You may have noticed that one-third of $315,000 is $105,000. Consider the extra $5,000 as a buffer for the firm's partnership to ensure profitability!) Thus, a rough equation of law firm economics is:

$$(Billing\ Rate\ *\ Min.\ Billable\ Hours\ Requirement)$$
$$/\ 3\ =\ Annual\ Salary$$

From the above, you should see that any of the three variables (billing rate, minimum billable hours requirement and salary) can be algebraically manipulated to make the equation work (*i.e.*, to assure the firm is profitable). For example, to increase your annual salary, while keeping the minimum billable hours requirement the same, your billing rate must be increased so as to not cut into the firm's (*i.e.*, the partnership's) profits. Therefore, you should now understand that as your salary goes up (*i.e.*, as a second-year, third-year, *etc.*), your billing rate consequently goes up, and you become more expensive to clients. The firm's rationale is that the more senior you become, the more value you provide to the client, thus justifying the higher billing rate. This "equation reality" results in an increased pressure to be more efficient the more senior you become.

The Jaguar® versus the Honda®

We've stated that practicing law is a business. Well you know that in order for a business to be profitable it must be run in a certain way. Unfortunately, however, there is not *one* certain way for all firms. Thus, your challenge is to learn how the business of practicing law is handled at your particular firm. You must eventually learn and understand: How are partners compensated? How are new clients cleared for conflicts? Do associates get any compensation for bringing in new clients to the firm (*i.e.*, "originating" clients?) How are bonuses calculated? How are individual associate raises determined? How are clients billed? The answers to all these law firm economics questions often determine how law is practiced at your particular firm.

Let's say you receive a legal research assignment and you need to decide whether you should do it "using the books" or whether you should use Westlaw. Well, how does Westlaw charge the firm?

Does the firm pass those charges on to the client? If so, can this client afford to pay? Is this a large client? Is this a small client? Does this client pay their bills? Will this client be willing to pay a large research-related bill? In sum, the reality of practicing law is that: *The amount of money the client has or is willing to spend affects how they are rendered legal counsel and the kind of legal services they receive.*

We'll now use an analogy that a senior partner once used to teach Raymond the above principle. A large corporate client can typically afford the "Jaguar sedan of patent applications," whereas an individual client with fewer resources may only be able to afford the "Honda Civic of patent applications." In some situations, however, even the client that can afford the Jaguar, only wants to pay for the Honda (if not the Yugo® coupe) of patent applications. Thus, what good is it for you to demonstrate your legal talent by building a Jaguar that the client cannot afford or is unwilling to pay for!? At the end of the day, you have not served the client because you have not given them what they wanted. (Think back to Chapter 3: you showed the *talent*, but what *image* have you created?)

The above is an example of where the business of practicing law affects the kind of legal services a client receives. Now, don't get us wrong. We are *not* saying that the client who can pay the most money, deserves most of your brainpower! Rather, we are saying that you must always do your best work, but it has to be within the resources the client can afford or is willing to spend. In other words, you have to do your best work in the amount of hours, given your billable rate, that the client can afford or that the client is willing to pay. To put this concept in mathematical terms, let's say a client only has or is only willing to spend $2,500 for obtaining legal services with respect to a particular project. If your billing rate is $175 per hour, you may think that you have approximately 14 hours to complete the project within budget (*i.e.*, 14 hours * $175 per hour = $2,450). Right? Wrong! What about the partner billing at $250 per hour who may need a couple of hours to review your work? What about any Westlaw charges, photocopying charges, *etc.*? These costs are real and must not be overlooked when planning "how much time can I spend on this project?"

Why Should You Care as an Associate?

We admit that, as a first-year or younger associate, your main concern should be learning the substantive practice of law and not worrying too much about efficiency, project budgets and partner compensation. However, your long-term goal may be to become an "equity partner." What is an equity partner? What does that mean? Well, being an equity partner is being part owner of the firm. It means being considered self-employed and sharing in the firm's profits (and losses). (Some firms also have what are called "service partners," "salary partners" or "non-equity partners." Just think of them as very senior associates with larger offices who are "equity-partners-in-training" or "equity-partners-in-waiting.")

Now as you go through the early part of your career at the firm, never lose sight of the equity partnership goal. Doing this will help you develop a business savvy about how to counsel and render legal services to clients. Why do this so early on? Well: *If you don't act like you own it, you never will!* In other words if your goal is to practice law at the firm, be successful and eventually become an equity partner, if you never act like an owner, you will never become one. Why should the partners vote you on as a part owner with them, when you've never demonstrated the savvy of an owner? Why should they want you to be their business partner if you don't know how to look out for the bottom line? Thus, not only must you become an expert in the substantive area of the law that you are practicing, but also eventually you have to learn that practicing law is a business and you have to "learn the business of practicing."

SIDEBAR TO NO. 10

Jorge A. Goldstein, Esq.
B.S. Rensselaer Polytechnic Institute; Ph.D., Harvard University;
J.D. George Washington University
Partner, Sterne, Kessler, Goldstein & Fox, PLLC, Washington, DC

Know Your Supervisors

I wholeheartedly agree with the suggestion that in your first years, you learn as much as possible about practicing law, especially how it is practiced in your firm. It is crucial that you learn how your supervising partners or supervising senior associates like things. No two lawyers are alike. I, for one, do not like my associates to put pen to paper until they have thoroughly discussed with me, face-to-face, the facts and the law of a project. In addition to giving me an opportunity to get to know them better, I can gauge their conclusions ahead of time and recommend that the memo, brief or letter they will generate either reflect those conclusions or a different set of conclusions—and how strongly the conclusions should be stated. That way, when I read the first draft, I already know what will be in it. Other supervisors want to see memos without meeting ahead of time. So, know your supervisors.

Know Their Budgetary Expectations and Talk About Them

One of the critical points about pleasing your supervisors is understanding their budgetary expectations. These, in turn, are controlled by the client for whom the work is being done. Is the matter on an open budget (*i.e.*, "money is no object, turn over every stone, leave nothing unexplored")? Or is the matter under a tight budget, or worse, a fixed fee (*i.e.*, "give me the best opinion you can for $2,500.00, including costs")? There is a very big difference between these two extremes and they require differing approaches on your part. You should understand at the outset that pretty much all legal engagements are budgeted and very few if any have a totally open-ended, "money is no object" approach. The question usually is: how tight is the budgetary requirement? Is it a general guideline or is it a strict limit?

Let's assume for starters that it is a strict limit. You might then feel that at your billing rate of $175, spending about 12–14 hours on the project will result in a mediocre job, and you may well be absolutely correct. You and your supervisor may even agree that a good job cannot be done in 12 hours, and yet the client insists on spending no more than $2,500.00. What do you do in such case? Whatever you do, you better discuss it with your supervisor ahead of time. One possibility is that you spend whatever time is needed to do a good job and your supervisor then bills the client no more than the $2,500.00 that the client budgeted. It is not uncommon for the firm to "take a haircut," as it is known. Good firms will not compromise the quality of their legal work and are willing to cut the bill so as to work within the budgetary constraints of a client. These firms' top reputations are the controlling factor.

If the strict budget is for a one-time project or for a limited few of them, but the client is an otherwise very profitable client, then the matter could be treated as a "loss leader." The firm would be willing to give a discount because it is receiving other very profitable work. If that is the case, then you must clarify with your supervisor that you will do a thorough job even if it takes more than 12–14 hours. And, your supervisor should agree on that. But you *must* discuss it beforehand so as to avoid the possible perception that you do not care about budgets or that you are inefficient—matters that might come up at review time.

If, however, a client constantly puts the firm—and you—under unreasonable monetary constraints, then the firm might ultimately decide that this is not a client that they want to serve, because constantly cutting bills results in an unprofitable business. So, what if the firm repeatedly asks that you work with very tight budgets? What should you do then?

Commodity vs. Bet the Company Work

It is useful at this stage that you recognize the different types of legal work as they have developed in the late 20th and early 21st centuries. Much legal work has become commoditized; that is, the competition for such work among law firms is based primarily on price. Much commoditized work is in fact on a fixed price per project. Examples of commoditized legal work include things like routine real estate closings, drafting certain types of patent applications, basic securities and banking matters, basic trusts and estates matters, and so on. Lawyers working on such matters need to be keenly aware that one of the reasons that the matters come to the firm has more to do with price and quick turnaround time than deep legal expertise and analyses. A firm may do commoditized matters if it can justify a large enough volume to make them profitable, or the firm may take them on as loss leaders so that it is situated favorably when the "bet the company" matters come around.

"Bet the company" matters, in contrast, are high value, (relatively) price insensitive legal engagements needing expertise, seasoning and proven track records. They might be things like merging two international companies in a complex legal and financial transaction, or litigating a massive antitrust case against the U.S. Government, or closing a real estate transaction on a piece of land in downtown Paris and in the process settling the estate of a deceased wine magnate. The "bet the company" cases are exciting, not the least because the client may have so much riding on the outcome that the cost—benefit calculations are quite one-sided (*i.e.*, the client cannot afford to lose). Keep in mind that with such cases come not only excitement and glory, but stress and pressure.

But please remember that most legal work is in fact under reasonable budgets and there is plenty of time for you to do a thorough job. I have chosen to expand here on both extremes so as to make a point.

Your Law Firm's Brand

To make matters even more interesting, a client may decide that it will send "bet the company work" to a different firm than the one that does its commoditized work. This may have to do with the client's perception that one firm is not equipped to handle large volumes of its repetitive work (or is too expensive to do so), and the other is equipped to handle only that. Of course, firms do not always see themselves as their clients see them. Firms may see themselves as being on the high end of things or capable of doing both types of work, while their clients do not see them that way. How the world perceives the firm is what we would call the "brand" of the firm—and this interesting topic could be the subject of an entirely different chapter . . . but that is for another day.

It is very important, as you are deciding where to work or how to deal with the work put in front of you, that you get a clear picture of the brand of your firm. You should always be willing to do price-sensitive work because you wish to impress on your supervising partner—who is *your* client within the firm, after all (everyone in this matrix has a client)—that you will do it as efficiently as possible and without complaint. This mirrors the wish of the partner to impress on the firm's client that her firm will do this work in hope of getting the "bet the company" case when it comes.

If, however, you perceive that the work that you do is never of the "bet the company" type, you might wish to ask yourself: Is it because the firm does not get such kind of work? If so, maybe you are not in the right kind of firm for you. Or, if the firm is getting such kind of work, but it does not seem to reach your desk, then maybe it's time to have a serious heart to heart with your supervisor. Maybe she has underestimated you, or maybe you have not proven yourself yet. Depending on the response you get, you might decide that your firm is not the best for you after all. (Or, maybe it is because you have in fact decided that you do not wish to assume the heavier burdens and responsibilities of "bet the company" work.)

Don't Worry ...

There are plenty of firms out there and, as evidenced by the dramatic increases in lawyers' salaries in the last few years, there is intense competition for you. You should be able to find the right combination of firm, supervisor, clientele and work to keep you busily employed—and happy—for years to come.

BONUS CHAPTER: FOR SUMMER ASSOCIATES ONLY

Welcome to the Promised Land! We're glad to see that those 3 a.m. study group cramming sessions paid off with good grades, and that the blue suit you bought for the interview worked nicely! You had a good vibe with the attorney who interviewed you and the questions you asked worked perfectly. (Do you think they know you asked the same questions at all your interviews?) You're in! You will spend your summer playing with the big boys and girls. You are likely to partake in many summer associate functions and multi-hour free lunches. You will have the feeling that you've got the whole world in your hands. There is one thing, however, that you don't have in your hands yet—a permanent offer!

We decided to write this special bonus chapter just for you because the transition from being a law student to a full-time associate starts, for most, during the summer after your second year of law school. Although a majority of the tips presented earlier in *From Finals to the Firm* will be helpful, we felt that there are some unique pitfalls to be avoided by summer associates. Therefore, we now present special tips just for you to ensure that your summer is a success (*i.e.*, you receive a permanent offer!)

Just in Case You Forget: You Don't Have the Job Yet!

A summer associate position is just a tryout. Thus, as you know, everyone who receives a tryout doesn't make the team. Your number one goal is to get a permanent offer regardless of whether you ultimately decide to accept it. (Life, after all, is all about having as many options as possible!) Firms are becoming a lot more selective in extending permanent offers to summer associates because of increasing pressure to be more efficient, leaner and more profitable. You don't want to be the one summer associate who doesn't receive a permanent offer. Nor do you want to be the one summer associate who receives an offer, but has left a bad impression with some of the attorneys you will work with upon returning in the Fall.

Regardless of whether there are rumors flying around the firm that not all of the summer associates will get offers, or that all of the summer associates will receive offers, you have to be your own angel. At the end of the day, which and what percentage of summer associates receive offers are based on many factors (merit, economics, *etc.*), some of which may be out of your control. Thus, we want to give you some tips to make sure that you maximize your summer associate opportunity while enjoying the summer.

Grow Gills—It's a Fishbowl!

Whether you're at a big or small firm for the summer, everyone from the secretaries to the managing partner is watching you. They are watching you all of the time. Do not be fooled by that social gathering at a partner's house, those two-hour lunches or the after-work happy hours. You are being evaluated in every setting in which firm people are present. This doesn't mean, however, that you have to be so reserved that you stifle your own personality. Your personality is EXACTLY what everyone is trying to figure out! Both your fellow summer associates and the firm's attorneys are trying to answer one question: "Am I going to like working with this person?" Everyone already assumes you don't know anything! So as long as you work diligently and put your best effort into each of your projects, you will be fine. The firm would not have invested in you by giving you the summer position if they didn't think that you were smart enough to do the work. So relax and be yourself. Letting your personality shine through the fishbowl as you work hard and work smart is one of the best things you can do.

Diamonds or Cubic Zirconias?

Most firms spruce up their appearance in preparation for the arrival of summer associates. Generally speaking, the larger or more prestigious the firm, the more hoopla and fantasy are going to be built into your summer experience (*i.e.*, they will present the so-called "summer cruise" version of law firm life). Attorneys at some firms tend to work less in the summer, so don't be fooled by the ability of associates and partners to hang out with you at happy hours and go on two-hour lunches. They are urged by management to hang out with summer associates during the summer! Try to weed out the things about the firm's environment that are only true while summer associates are present.

The weeding out process involves asking questions such as: Do associates really hang out socially during the non-summer months? Are partners usually willing to spend an hour explaining a new assignment or do they usually just "dump and run"? Is it common to actually work with partners or are new associates usually paired with senior (or even junior) associates? Summertime is usually a slower period of the year, so people are working less and feeling better about life because of the longer periods of daylight. By letting your personality shine and getting to know people well enough to ask questions, find out what life is like during the rest of the year. Ask them whether the casual, laid-back "vibe" of the firm, where no one is pulling all-nighters and no one seems stressed is an accurate reflection of the year-round firm environment. In sum, you want to know what's real about the firm (*i.e.*, diamonds) and what's not real, but just looks real (*i.e.*, cubic zirconias).

Watch Them Just Like They're Watching You!

If your number one goal is to get an offer, your number two goal should be to figure out whether you really like the firm and will eventually accept the offer. You should focus on two things: The firm's *people* and the firm's *potential*.

The People

The factors that will most affect your happiness at the firm will be the people who work there and the environment that they foster. Do you like the people you will be working with? You may mostly be paired with senior associates and partners in the summer, and you should ascertain whether you like their style of supervision and interaction. But you should do your best to also interact with your fellow summer associates and the youngest current associates. Most associates will tell you that their support group and closest friends come from the group of new associates who walked in the door with them or the associate class right before them. If you don't see yourself developing a good rapport with anybody in these two groups, you should take a hard look at whether the people at the firm fit the type of people with whom you want to spend 10–12 hours per day.

Analyzing the people should also include analyzing the overall environment of the firm. You should start by assessing the things you like or dislike about the work environment. Any question you ask (and ultimately answer) about the firm should be compared to your desires for an ideal work environment. For example, if the firm is a high-pressure, highly-competitive environment where people work long hours and spend no time socializing, you need to know whether you can, and want to, fit into that kind of environment. Maybe you want to work in a more laid-back environment. Ask yourself whether you like the way people interact at the firm. How do the partners treat the associates? How do the associates treat each other? Do you have a sense that people get to know each other or do they just work hard and go home? Which do you prefer? How do the attorneys treat the staff? (You care about this because, as we pointed out in Chapter 4, *the staff is it*!) Do you have priorities outside of the office that you don't want to sacrifice? Different firms value your free time differently. Some firms only allow associates enough free time to sleep, shower and eat. Other firms put a premium on allowing lawyers to balance their careers and their personal lives. Many fall somewhere in the middle. What are your priorities?

The Potential

Beyond getting to know and understand the people and environment of the firm, you must learn as much as you can about your potential to grow at the firm. Will you have opportunities to build your "talent," foster a great "image" and gain the necessary "exposure?" Is the firm a "sink-or-swim" environment where you receive a lot of responsibility early on, but no guidance or mentoring? Is that the type of environment in which you will thrive? Is the firm the type of place where associates work for years on menial tasks for big projects before they gain marketable legal skills? Talk to associates who are in their first, second and third years at the firm. Ask them what type of assignments they are receiving. Ask them how much mentoring and teaching they received along the way. Compare their answers with the type of environment you think you will need in order to be successful.

The types of work that are available at the firm also determine your potential. Does the firm have significant work in the practice areas in which you're interested? For example, just because a firm advertises that it has a "Labor and Employment Group" doesn't mean the group is thriving enough to keep you busy once you become an associate at the firm! Moreover, does the group do the type of work in which you are interested? You must go below the surface when analyzing any of the firm's departments. Analyze the dominant client base and work product of the department. For example, the firm's Real Estate Group may mostly represent landlords and lenders, yet you want to represent tenants and borrowers. You may want to do commercial litigation, but the firm's litigation group is mostly a white-collar criminal practice.

Lastly, try to get a sense of which departments are the "hottest" at the firm. There are many indications that may reveal whether a department is highly regarded at the firm. These indications include: Which departments generate the most revenue? Which departments are growing and have lots of new partners? Which departments seem to be receiving most of the firm's resources? Does a certain department have all of the firm's "stars" (*i.e.*, the most well-respected associates and partners)? You want to make sure that the department you're coveting at the firm not only has a future for *you*, but that it has a future *at the firm*. It is much more difficult to be considered a very successful associate at the firm (and almost impossible to become a partner) if you are part of a stagnant, resource-depleted department filled with associates and partners who are not considered to be an important part of the firm's future growth and success.

The City and Your Friends

Once you become a full-time associate, you will be a member of a department that is within a firm, which is within a building, which is on a block within a neighborhood, which is within a city! Do not get so caught up in your analysis of the people and the potential at the firm that you forget to figure out whether you like the city where you will work! It is very important for you to go around town and check out different neighborhoods, go out socially to the dance clubs and the bars to see whether you'd like living as a working adult in that city. This is true regardless of whether you grew up in that city. You may find that you like your firm, but the city is too slow (or too fast) for your chosen lifestyle. If you have specific hobbies or cultural or religious activities that are important to you, make sure that you can partake in those activities in the firm's city. For example, if you love outdoor activities such as hiking or mountain biking, make sure that the city in which you'll be working will accommodate those interests. You want to choose a city that, when you do have precious free time, will be able to fulfill and satisfy your non-work desires.

Lastly, don't forget to talk to any friends you have who are summer associates at other firms. You should share in their experiences. This is particularly true if you are a summer associate at a firm after your first year of law school—you will have the opportunity to try another firm next year and it would be good to get information from friends while it's still fresh in their minds! Have no shame—if there's a happy hour thrown by another firm (and it does not cause you to miss an event *your* firm is hosting) you should go to it just to get a feel for the people. You may find that one of your friends is working at a firm that has the type of people and potential more suitable for you than your own firm. Be careful, however, because your best bet to understanding a firm is through your own experience. But, your friends can give you good information that will assist you in assessing the firm you work for during the summer so that you have a balanced perspective. For example, you may think that your firm was a "sweatshop" because everyone seemed to work so hard in the corporate group. After polling your fellow summer associate friends at other firms, however, you find out that *every* corporate group works long hours. Therefore, this tells you that going to another firm to do corporate work may not get you a slower pace than the pace you experienced at your firm.

Don't Worry, Be Happy!

All in all, have fun! The more fun you have, the more you'll relax, and the more your personality, which is a very important part of a firm's evaluation of you, will shine through. This is not to say that you should not work hard to do your best on each assignment—consistently poor reviews on your projects will prevent you from getting an offer regardless of how much everyone likes you.

Your ability to produce a quality work product is much more important than being a social butterfly. If you need to skip a summer associate function to do a high-quality job on an assignment, skip the function. Or, if possible, go to the summer event for a short period of time and then return to the office to finish the assignment. You may also opt to do some of the work over the weekend when things are quieter at the office. Don't be fooled into thinking that all of the other summer associates are slacking, or that they are not going the extra mile in order to do high-quality work. Never forget that the firm attracts, breeds and is filled with attorneys who are hard-working, driven and smart. Those same types of people are in your summer associate class and are working hard to submit high-quality work, regardless of how many margaritas you see them toss back during the firm barbecue at the partner's house!

In addition, doing high-quality work on a smaller number of assignments is better than taking on a large number of assignments and doing average or poorly on them. Your performance evaluation can only be based on the assignments you complete. Thus, it is important to do well on those completed assignments, rather than billing an enormous amount of hours on a large number of projects, each with mediocre results. The firm's hiring committee already assumes you will bill a lot of hours when you get to the firm—everyone does! Sadly enough, your ability to work 70 hours a week is not in question while you are a summer associate. It is your ability to produce high-quality work on challenging projects for demanding clients and supervisors which is the key factor being evaluated. So don't take on new assignments when your intuition tells you it will cause the work product on previously-assigned projects to suffer. As a wise senior associate once advised Calvin: *"They'll never remember the projects you didn't take!"*

As for completed assignments, ask for feedback directly from your supervisors to make sure you are on the right track. You do not want to go through the summer thinking everything is great only to find out that you have done poorly on a number of assignments. As we discussed earlier, take part in as many social activities as you can stand so that you can get an accurate reflection of the "people" and the "potential" of the firm. You are a summer associate and indeed, despite not yet having an offer, the world is your oyster because you have been given an *opportunity*. Seize that opportunity by the horns and ride, ride, ride. And, have a few frozen margaritas on the firm while you're at it!

Plan B

What happens if, through no fault of your own (or maybe it was your fault), you don't receive an offer? Well, it's time for "Plan B"! Actually, the first part of Plan B should be put into place well before you find out that you didn't receive an offer. That is, *never assume you will get an offer and fail to sign up for your law school's on-campus interview program!* Next, you want to find out why you didn't receive an offer—as we mentioned in Chapter 9, go get the belt! It is best to do this as soon as you are informed of your "no offer" status. This is important not only so that you can identify the areas you need to improve upon, but also so you're prepared to answer this question as it will come up in later interviews with other firms.

You also want to work closely with your law school's career development or career placement office whose functions include handling these situations. They can help you in doing "damage control" and getting your career back on the right track. Such damage control involves contacting a partner or senior associate for whom you did good work during the summer to ask them if they are willing to be a reference for you when you apply to other firms or legal employers. In the end, not receiving an offer is not the end of the world. It may just mean that particular firm was not the right fit for you, law firm life is not the lifestyle for you, or, just simply, that particular firm did not do a good job in matching the size of their summer associate class with their full-time new associate hiring needs. This is the time to be the CEO of your career!

ENDNOTE: NEVER CROSS THE LINE!

We've been happy to share with you our top ten things new associates should know. While we attempted to make our top ten informative, inspirational and insightful, we would be remiss if we did not add just one more tip. (We figured that "Top Eleven" would not have been as catchy in a title as "Top Ten," so consider the following tip a bonus.)

As you begin your law firm career as an associate, you will be attempting to do several things including finding an angel, being your own angel, T.I.E.ing, C.Y.A.ing, and J.U.S.T. A.S.K.ing. However, you must always remember to never "touch the line" (yet alone cross it). That is, you must always strive to stay on the correct side of the line of ethical conduct and professional responsibility. Unlike in baseball, hitting the foul line as long as you don't completely cross over it is *not* a fair ball!

During law school, you may have heard the old adage that: *Should there ever be a time when it looks like either you or your client may go to jail, make sure it is your client.* As good of advice as this may be, allow us to add a corollary: *Should there ever be a time when it looks like either you or the partner you work for may be disbarred, make sure it isn't you!* Always be aware that:

> A lawyer is bound by the Rules of Professional Conduct notwithstanding that the lawyer acted at the direction of another person.

"Responsibilities of a Subordinate Lawyer," Rule 5.2(a) of the ABA Model Rules of Professional Conduct (2002).

One scholar, over a decade ago, observed:

> As the lives of senior lawyers—particularly those in the elite firms—become dominated by the pursuit of billable hours, and as the lives of law professors—particularly those in the elite schools—become dominated by the pursuit of published pages of scholarship, both lawyers and law professors are turning their backs on much else that is important. And among the most critical of the responsibilities that senior lawyers and law professors are abandoning is the moral formation of the young—the shaping of law students and new lawyers into ethical practitioners.[7]

---

7. Patrick J. Schiltz, *Legal Ethics in Decline: The Elite Law Firm, the Elite Law School, and the Moral Formation of* the Novice Attorney, *82 Minn. L. Rev. 705, 706–07 (Feb. 1998).*

Put in other words, it is up to you to be your own angel! Thus, you have to: (a) become familiar with the rules of professional conduct for the jurisdiction(s) in which you practice; and (b) as you professionally mature and develop a specialty, take advantage of Continuing Legal Education (CLE) classes to become aware of the common ethical pitfalls that attorneys within your specialty frequently encounter.

Regardless of the great number of attorneys you may personally know, the profession is still a tight circle where word gets around. (This is true even among clients.) As an attorney (*i.e.*, a member of the bar) involved in the business of practicing law, your most important assets are your word and your reputation. When you promise something to a client by a certain date, you must deliver on time. Don't make promises you know beforehand that you can't keep. Should there ever be a time when it looks like you have to break a promise (*e.g.*, miss a deadline), a telephone call to that effect should be made by you as soon as possible, not after the deadline has passed. Likewise, when you say (or represent) something is true, it should be the truth. When a partner or senior associate relies on you to research a legal issue, the information you provide them to use in counseling a client should be reliable. Put simply, ethical and professional responsibility lapses will tarnish your image and result in the wrong type of exposure.

No matter how much you implement the top ten things as a From Finals to the Firm veteran, failure to conduct yourself ethically and represent your clients responsibly will not result in success. To put it in economic terms (being your own CFO), a loss of your license to practice law (or even suffering damage to your professional reputation) can severely hamper your ability to repay your student loans, pay your mortgage or even pay that fancy car note.

In sum: ***Be dependable and be honest, or be something other than a practicing attorney!***

†